"I'm Here" Proclaims A Little Girl Who Was Not Allowed to Be

A First - Person Narrative of Abuse, Trauma,Dissociation and Healing

by 'Reace

Order this book online at www.trafford.com
or email orders@trafford.com

Most Trafford titles are also available at major online book retailers.

Printed in the United States of America.

ISBN: 978-1-4269-6044-4 (sc)
ISBN: 978-1-4269-6043-7 (hc)
ISBN: 978-1-4269-6042-0 (e)

Library of Congress Control Number: 2011903450

Trafford rev. 04/27/2011

 www.trafford.com

North America & International
toll-free: 1 888 232 4444 (USA & Canada)
phone: 250 383 6864 ♦ fax: 812 355 4082

TABLE OF CONTENTS

DEDICATION

To the little girl inside of me. She is here and I honor her with love and gratitude for hanging onto her package of light and love that is truly magical.

And to my sweet grand-daughter who has taught me it really is okay to get mad, tell people how she feels and play again. She brings great joy to me.

To my two sons, for their continuing love, I feel truly blessed.

ACKNOWLEDGMENTS

First, I'd like to thank my dear friend, Beverley, who volunteered to edit this book. At the time I was journaling, she said she would edit it if I ever decided to publish. With these acknowledgements and the Introduction, she often asked me questions to find the deeper significance of an experience and was able to express my thoughts and feelings with greater clarity. (She surprised herself to realize she's also a ghost writer!) Beverley also guided me through the publishing process.

Thank God for Ernie, who came to the church to get my boys and I the day my ex-husband almost murdered me! And for Ernie's wife, Zandra, who opened her home for us to stay for the first three months. My deepest thanks.

To Sandra Sammartino, my Restorative Yoga Teacher/ Trainer. Her Yoga was a significant part of my healing process.

To my therapist Bob Berger, who I trusted with my life and continue to do so. I felt held inside of his great white wings as if I were a precious little bird, held in a way that a space was reserved just for me, never feeling held against my will and always with room to move and explore. He is now an old friend.

In my first year of therapy, Bob asked me to draw a picture of how I saw myself. I drew a straight line with a circle on top. Artist Richelle Grist, in her cover illustration, gave me form! She was also able to express compassion in my adult face. My inner child is looking up at me with adoration! Wow! It touches both sadness and awe that my little one could love me that much. It's truly a beautiful picture. To Richelle my deepest heartfelt thanks!

And it is with delight that I thank my darling grand-daughter, whom I'd asked to help grandma out. She sat at my desk and ever so seriously printed, "I'm here". She was so proud to participate. My grand-daughter is the same age as my little one was when she insisted, "I'm here!"

To Dr. Rick Bradshaw who accepted me into his study in One Eye Integration even though my level of trauma was so huge. I felt so completely accepted for who I was. Wow, this was huge for me! I continue to feel treated with respect and appreciation for all of what I have learned from my life experience. He now thinks of me as a friend and colleague. I'm still integrating that!

To my college instructor, Lorna Kirkham, who went above and beyond by getting permission from the College for me to design my own practicum: developing second stage housing for abused women and their children. She is also now a dear friend.

To my family Doctor, Dr. Wayne Baker for all the external as well as internal bandages.

And to all my other friends along my healing journey.

Thank you! I love you all.

FOREWORD

"It occurred to me that this would undoubtedly be a profound story, because you are a profound person, 'Reace! For that reason I set out to chronicle my responses and reactions as I read... (see below)."
– Rick Bradshaw, PhD, Rpsych, May 2009.

Feelings of Awe and Respect.
As I move beyond the preamble, qualifications, and introduction, I notice a poetic, even spiritual quality to the writing.... "They are all a part of my life and the people I heard in the distance as a child".

What profound terror and sadness you had to endure as such a young and sensitive child - so loving and caring and generous and innocent - and made to witness, even participate in, the torture and killing of those you loved (animals and little friends). You were surrounded by *monsters*!

Feelings of Anger and Sadness.
Yet in the midst of that horror your spirit touched *wonder*, almost imperceptibly, in reverse... like you were hiding in God's robe, from the evil that was seeking to corrupt and destroy you soul. In that place you found warmth and wholeness...amazing!

...Atrocities - cult members, hidden from view, emerge at full moons to abuse innocent children, trying to separate them from their own souls, dumping their own shame...

Yes - so strong, and so caring in your heart and spirit, yet in your body unable to make them stop, and no one to help you – *alone* with monsters!...

Great to see your nurturing selfcare for your wounded child selves... the internal validation and comforting...the soothing of the painful body memories...

I'm so intrigued by your self-reflections, your ability to stand outside and look back at your adult and child and current lives...and re-think, re-evaluate, re-member...You "walked into the shadow of death and returned, without fearing evil..."

Such powerful insights - about how your father made you feel sorry for him - as if *he* was the "victim" and at the same time dumping the shame for his outrageous acts on you - but, thank God, it didn't stick! It's *his stuff*, not yours to carry! You can walk free and hold your head high - you got your boys out of an abusive situation, at the cost of (almost) your own life - and you helped hundreds of *other* women in those same circumstances, by starting the second - stage transition homes.

Profound plays on words :

*in - curable*_= curable from inside

in - sane = go in to become sane

Rick Bradshaw, Ph.D.
Registered Psychologist
Associate Professor &
Community Counselling Coordinator
Graduate Program in Counselling Psychology
Trinity Western University

INTRODUCTION

"**SOME STORIES AREN'T MEANT TO BE TOLD**", this is what they tried to convince me of. Or maybe I should say, brainwashed me of.

"I'm here, I'm here", she says.

For she truly is here, right here inside of me looking out, participating with excitement.

"I can tell now, I can tell now".

Yes little girl, you can tell now, no one is going to hurt you if you tell. It's OK to tell what you need to tell.

She takes a big breath and her timidness is apparent, but that's OK. I'm not in a hurry; I'm not going anywhere.

"I'm afraid and I'm scared 'Reace. Don't let them hurt me; please don't let them hurt me. I hurt, I hurt 'Reace. Please stop and hold me for a moment".

Okay, I will.

Twenty years later and I remember hearing this little girl inside of me. I side-stepped a lot to avoid the pain that I felt when I connected with her. She is the strong one. She says it's okay, we'll be okay. We *are* okay and alive. We can take care of each other.

I want to acknowledge her strength, my strength and so I've decided to call this book "*I'm Here*", I was the little girl who was not allowed to be and I AM HERE. They could not kill me.

I not only hear her, I can see her inside of my self as she pulls at my jeans and I look down to smile at her. I can hear you, little one. It took me a long time to hear and see what you lived through. It hurts my heart to see what you lived through and I am here for you, for me. WE are alive and so sad, so many tears of healing to feel now.

This has been a difficult journey for me, and a hard place to get to, to be psychologically ready to share my story. Sharing my story is exciting yet terrifying because some of the people I wrote about are still alive.

Until I wrote this journal, I never understood, in such a clear way, why I had wanted so desperately for my life to be over.

After the first or second year in therapy, I remembered that when I was 14, I attempted suicide. I wanted someone to run me over. (I didn't try and slice my arm like my mom did when we lived up North.)

I was walking down the middle of 7th avenue wanting a car to hit me. It was late and dark outside. I was crying very hard. My dad had just had sex with me again and I was feeling so dirty and wanted it to all be over. One man opened his car window and called me a crazy kid and yelled go home you stupid kid. If only he knew why I was doing what I was trying to do.

On this night I decided as I cried out to God, I'll show them, I'll show them all. I will get an in-curable disease and then I will find a cure for it. Then someone WILL see me.

I forgot that I had made this conscious decision. And then I began to write this journal and re-member and understand why I manifested Multiple Sclerosis.

When I was 16 or 17, I started having black out spells and no one knew why. When I was 23 I lost the sight in my left eye shortly after the birth of my first son; when I was 24 I lost the sight in my right eye shortly after the birth of my second son. Both times were a three month process of losing and then regaining sight. These are MS symptoms!

(2009, I *now know that I lost the sight in my left eye because this is where I stored my childhood trauma. I locked it in my right brain and covered it in a pillow-like substance called plaque so I could not see the trauma. This is similar to how I healed my foot that has the eye end of a sewing needle in it that I'd stepped on.(X-rays of my foot still show the needle surrounded by a pillow-like substance!*)

Sometimes, while journaling, the little girl comes out during the recollection and I allow her to write. She has a voice now. I have a voice now and I like to let her, who is in me, speak for herself. As I give myself permission to do this, I grow inside myself and become more whole and sensitive. And so, you will become aware of the many changes in the writings. It was very healing for the adult me to allow her to release, to sob and to type *her* story.

My now adult life triggers the memories of my childhood. I'm getting in touch with how my body reacts to different situations; I pay attention and listen to what my body is trying to tell me. I find it interesting how much I have learned just paying attention to how my body responds to the many different life experiences that I have.

As an adult, I have had many traumatic memories come through my unconscious to my conscious mind, which are of occult rituals that I went through when I was a child. At long last I feel safe enough, I *am* safe enough to remember.

As I wrote in my journal each morning I stated this intent, "*I am open, my unconscious mind is completely conscious, I am extremely prosperous/wealthy and I am full of love.*"

The memories will continue to come for me and I am strong enough to cope now. I no longer have the need to dissociate from parts of my body. I take the memory trauma to my therapy sessions to release it. I go into the trauma feeling through my body, deep into the tissues through awareness of my breath. This leaves me feeling exhausted yet more whole.

When I was a little girl, I used to look into my eyes in the mirror. I would leave my body through my eyes and go into the eyes in the mirror. My mirror eyes would then look back out into the eyes of the little girl outside. I'd go back and forth until I disappeared. I discovered that this was magical. Many years later, I realized it helped me stay alive because I didn't have to feel what was happening to me. By becoming totally amnesiac, I was able to survive.

When I discovered someone who like me, believes that our eyes are the doorway into our memories, I felt so very validated. This person is Dr. Rick Bradshaw with whom I did One Eye Integration. He or one of his interns, while making a sweeping motion with two fingers, tracked my eye movements which helped to release the blocks that I had for such a long time in my vision. My dissociation showed up in my eyes. As the blocks were opened, grief poured out of me.

This experience also helped me reconnect with the different dissociated parts of myself that I felt incapable of living with due to the trauma.

I had a friend who could not cope with her memories. Sometimes when she remembered parts of her past, she ended up in the psychiatric unit at the hospital. Sometimes I used to think I should check in to the psychiatric unit. But I always managed to get clear, to be present here in the now.

I don't know if I have enough time left in this life to reconnect all the parts of myself that I disconnected from due to my earlier life.

In 1989 I went to a week long summer intensive camp, co-facilitated by Starhawk and shared what I had begun to write of this journal (to June 30, 1989.) She kept the copy for 3 days and then came to me 3 times. Each time she had something different to say.

The first: "I have more faith in humankind".

The second: "I found reading what you've written a very healing experience".

The third: "I urge you to continue writing just the way that you are".

With Starhawk's feedback plus support from my loving friends, especially Ernie and Zandra and their family, and the love of my two little sons, I persevered.

This story is my memories of my own experience from my point of view.

I would like my life experience to not be in vain, for my story to help people and, especially, to educate those who work with abused, traumatized, dissociated individuals and assist with *their* healing. You can make a difference. **I can make a difference**.

THE JOURNAL

May 25, 1989 "Reace" is born. A new name and a new sense of courage.

The life of 'Reace (in part)

A place to begin; I'm not quite sure where to start; I guess this is a start. I'm feeling excited inside about the thought of actually considering putting my story down on paper. So many people write their stories, but mine is definitely unique. I should not by rights be alive today. I am aware of, everyone has a unique story.

There is magic in the air right now. As the night settles in, calmness grows inside of myself. Not so long ago when the night came, I would go away and hide inside of me. I did not know the place and it was so far away.

It is incredible how a small child can create a place so powerful that the soul and spirit cannot be touched. Such is the magic of life.

Today, as I prepare for the magic of the dream world, I do so with the excitement of wonder. What will the dream world teach me, show me and give me this night?

The place I found inside of me to live in, I lived there throughout the day also. I created a world of illusion that was so strong that no one being could any longer touch me. My world was full of dolls that had life, these dolls I gave names to. Still today, I have these dolls in my bedroom on the headboard of my bed. These dolls are all special; they all represent a part of me, precious parts of a little girl who was not allowed to be.

I remember a lot of times now because it is safe enough to remember. As I sit here in this chair typing, the magic grows even stronger. I'm beginning to unlock a door inside, as if it is meant to be that this magic is happening. I knew that one day I would begin to tell my story. Unique, but everyone is unique, a part of me says. I have all of these voices that have thoughts that need to be put down on this paper and so I will include them. They are all a part of my life and the people I heard in the distance as a child.

Who would ever think that a little girl who was not, would grow up and be a powerful woman (women tell me I am powerful, I feel very vulnerable) who is president of a feminist society and the developer of a second stage transition house. Maybe this is why it is finally safe enough to tell the story I have to tell. Credibility I now have, yes, that makes sense, I have credibility now and no person can dismiss me as a nut case. God was I ever brainwashed. I just got that; I was programmed to think that if I ever told, no one would believe me.

It's as if the life that I remember belongs to someone else, almost like I am watching a movie of a story I find hard to believe is true. A world within a world within a world, how true! I know those worlds exist, I know because I lived in that world. People go to watch horror shows and I wonder if they realize that the story just might be true.

When I was little, a little dolly, I told someone once. They said, little girls should not tell stories like that and they told my mom what I said. My mom said to them that she would make sure that I didn't say those things again. I never told anyone ever again. I found a place further away inside of me and didn't come out again until I was 34 years old.

I spent a long time away inside of me. When I came out so very far, at first it was hard to find the middle because I came out so far. Now I can be out and I can be in, so many people would like to be able to do this. I can fly when I'm out and in at the same time. I feel balanced when I am in this place inside of me. But with this balance come a pain so strong and sadness so great.

May 26, 1989

My dreams were mixed last evening. There was a dog in one dream and she was being chopped apart. In the dream I saw the dog I have now, but I know it wasn't her because I was little in the dream. I can't remember the entire dream because it was a horror sort of dream. There was a man and I think it was my father of origin. I was wide eyed in the dream, almost bug eyed with terror.

There were two parts of me, one part that helped the man skin and a part that did nothing but watch in terror. He took the left leg and hip off and threw it onto the fire to cook and it still had all the hair on it; that moment I was present and looked at the dog. The dog was alive when the man did this and the dog looked at me with so much sadness. Before I became present I had a sense that I was helping the man by skinning the parts that he gave to me.

It's as if a door opened last night and this memory was released, or maybe it is a sign of what I will be getting myself into as I make this journey into this story. At this moment I give myself permission to stop whenever I need to. The sign being chopping the animal in me apart and throwing the pieces into the fire, hair and all. That would be the gestalt way of looking at it.

I acknowledge the dance of avoidance I do as I prepare to journey into the past that I have run so hard to get away from. And yet, I'm pulled to acknowledge that little girl who was not allowed to be.

May 27, 1989

I am not quite 39 earth years and yet I am tired, so very tired. I walk in a world that is not as any others; my world is not as rushed as others are. When I work I accomplish much more than others, so I am told. So many try to give away their inadequacies by saying, you make me feel instead of saying, I feel! How many are willing to be responsible for their thoughts, their actions and their acts!!!

I am full of anger and a fire that burns ever so strong inside of me. My rage is an emotion that has been the undercurrent of my successes, my will, my light and my motivation to live. I thank the Goddess for this. I never though that I would appreciate anger, the emotion that I feared to the depths of my soul and yet this emotion has kept me alive. Isn't it interesting that what I feared the most is what I could not face inside of myself? What bothers me in another is what I was not okay with inside of me.

This wisdom I have is curious to me. In writing down my story, I am becoming clearer about my own thoughts and in the meaning of life. Life is a dance, an expression of the self and we are all doing it!

I have been outside of myself for a few years now, but find the need to go inside of me once more. When I go out to meet people I am open and vulnerable. It is as if I do not exist because I am just here, clear. The newness is that I can be inside of me and see out at the same time. I am home in my house inside of me. I have traveled so far only to arrive at the beginning and know it for the first time. One hell of a journey!!

There is warmth inside of a full feeling, completeness and me. And so I begin. Again and again and again. The life of a little girl who was not allowed to be.

"I'm here, I'm here", she says.

For she truly is here, right here inside of me looking out, participating with excitement.

"I can tell now, I can tell now".

Yes little girl, you can tell now, no one is going to hurt you if you tell. It's OK to tell what you need to tell.

She takes a big breath and her timidness is apparent, but that's OK. I'm not in a hurry; I'm not going anywhere.

"I'm afraid and I'm scared 'Reace. Don't let them hurt me; please don't let them hurt me. I hurt, I hurt 'Reace. Please stop and hold me for a moment".

Okay, I will.

I love you little one, I love you and you can tell when it is all right for you. I know how much you hurt; your tears come out of my eyes. It's OK to cry and it's OK to be scared.

Later

My little one has curled up for awhile. There is a large pain in my chest and a choking sensation in my throat. I know that this journey of validation is going to be an ever-painful time.

I can cry for me and allow myself to grieve for all of the ugly times that on my journey I was raped, abused, used and subjected to destruction. I truly am a wonder.

"Star light star bright, magic and dreams is here now".

Little ditties I always said to cheer me up. Isn't it wonderful how we humans can protect ourselves? Just think of something different, distract us.

I'm feeling the need to set up an anchor for myself so that I don't get lost into the pain and sorrows of the past. The abuse happened a long time ago, it is not now. It was then. My work with the second stage transition house, my two sons, being president of a feminist society, the animals, my colleagues and my friends are anchors for me.

I started to remember, I guess I was somewhere between 11 and 13. Anyway, I didn't know that I was remembering, I just thought I was having these horrible nightmares. Night after night I dreamed of people in dark robes like monks robes, coming all around me in my room to get me. I would soak my bed with sweat. I could not scream, I could not call out. There was no sound there, no voice. I wanted to cry out but I could not. They would come and get me, night after night and take me to this place. I would be placed on a table in the center of this room. There were candles everywhere in the room.

When I was 16 or 17 I started having black out spells and no one knew why. When I was 23 I lost the sight in my left eye (shortly after the birth of my first son) and then in my right eye when I was 24 (shortly after the birth of my 2nd. Son).

Please God, I would beg, just give me one day without the pain! As a child I would scratch myself until I bled during my sleep. This would make mother angry because I got blood on her white sheets.

I need to stop for tonight because I am getting light headed and a little dizzy.

May 28, 1989

Today I spent rewriting what I've already written because I need to give my words more space. Yesterday, when I talked about being in that room on the table, well, sometimes they just left me there tied up. My brother, Donald, would sneak a drink of water in to me. He took a big chance doing that. I thought so at the time. What he did would give me something so special to hang on to. He was so scared, but still he would come with the water. I was 5 years old and he was 3. Two babes who were trying to survive.

One time after they'd had their funny moaning service, there were some pieces of me on the table between my legs. I put them back inside.

May 29, 1989

Today I went to visit my friend. When she was little she had a dad who did things to her. I met her about 4 years ago and since then, the little girl in me has felt like she truly has a friend, someone who really knows that deep annihilation. Where we are at, inside of ourselves, at that moment in time, is whom we attract.

I could not grow inside until my little person had a friend, had recognition for being alive. Her father had similar ceremonies; we both got put inside of coffins for the sick service. SICK does not do it justice. People who can do those things and fall asleep at night! I cannot comprehend. It is so crazy making, repulsive and Goddess I cannot find a word that truly gives this form of behaviour its measure.

I've spent years doing my own therapy around my childhood. I worked with a woman Psychiatrist for two and a half years and in this time began to grow into the adult that I said I would never grow into. Adults were mean and vicious. My mother was someone I never wanted to grow into. She was ugly inside. The woman I worked with and my friends showed me that not all women were ugly. No wonder I could not grow up, I did not have a model. I learned more from men as a child. (As an adult I can look back and see the pain my mother had inside of herself. If she were alive today I would hold her and tell her I understand her survival techniques.)

I did get some attention from my father, even if he had a part that was mean and a part that was okay. There was this nice daddy who would be so wonderful and gentle, I loved this daddy. This father was the only one that I consciously saw and the other one, the one I denied existed, was hurtful and mean. The evil one was the one who abused me sexually and ritually.

Now as an adult with all of this education that I've integrated, I can see why I have so many of the behaviour patterns that I do.

June 1,1989

The deeper the water the more still it becomes. There is so much pain inside of me, so very much pain. I've been so very busy in the material world. The more I hurt, the more work I tend to do.

Yet I've not been as attached to my material work of late as I normally am. I feel distant, not as focused, as I usually tend to be. My eyes burn with the tears that I still need to shed. I should be happy, well I am truly happy for myself and all of my accomplishments but I don't stop hurting. What can be justice for the cruelties that were done?

When my mother said she'd fix it so that I would not say those things again, well, she put me in the closet, a little closet that was dark. I was told I'd stay there until I learned never to say ugly lies again.

"But they weren't lies 'Reace! They weren't lies they really did those things to me".

Mother left me in the closet for a long time, so long that the only thing to drink was my urine. I curled up in the corner vowing never to share again and now as I share on paper I can hardly see. The tears are interfering with my sight.

Today I went up to the newspaper to have my picture taken to go into the paper with a report on my second-stage housing. I was distant and unattached to the people I was being introduced to. It is so very hard to let me take any glory or credit for anything that I do. What will it take to balance this pain? What will it take to tip the scale to the other side? Is there a power on this planet that can give me the love that it will take to help me balance this pain? Is there?

I do not run any more. (It's just turned 2009 and I say, who am I trying to kid re the run thing?) Maybe this good stuff is making me hurt so much? Even though I was distant when I was getting my picture taken, I was still there, watching and seeing a little bit. The good stuff comes in and some old hurts my little girl has, come out. At least now I'm getting in some good things. Before I would not let nice things come into my space, only bad. For I believed that I was evil, I believed that I was responsible for all the wicked things that I supposedly caused just because I was born a little girl.

For such a long time I'd wished I were a boy and then none of those things would have happened. I even married a man who liked little boys. So, I would stay skinny and keep my hair cut real short just to keep him in my bed. Besides, who wanted to be a girl anyway? Not I!! Not then anyway. Today I love to be a woman. I've filled out my body and grown my hair, I wear dresses and skirts almost every day and I love my femininity. (And now in 2009, I wear slacks and sneakers to work in.)

There is always this feeling of curiosity in me. I can see myself sitting on a riverbank, watching life flow on and on, my life, and right now I am observing it. I find it interesting to watch and feel. I know that I am not going anywhere really because there is nowhere to go. (I'm out of my body in this place.)

I suppose I've moved on. There is no need to stay in that old life, life flows on, ever moving, ever changing like that river I watch flow by.

We can set a stage once we have been able to step out of life. I suppose right now I'm on the outside of life looking in at whether or not I really want to get back in.

Remembering comes in little bits at a time, thank God. When I first began opening the door I relived being penetrated by a full-grown man. I was three and a half years old. My body was ripped and torn open. I remembered leaving my body and then an angel came. I

9

know now that I split myself into more than one. How else would I have survived? I still have yet to integrate the little girl who knew that awful daddy. I have some recall of sexual acts that happened. In the night I wake crying, "Please daddy stop, please daddy I don't want to do that, it hurts when you do that ."

And then the silent screams. I sit in the corner of my room with my pink elephant, where it is safe to cry and cuddle. When I was little I used to sit in the corner and cry. I could feel safe in the corner. God knows why. I wasn't safe anywhere.

More and more the memories come from the little girl who knew that awful daddy. I guess she is here inside of me.

Denial! "Sometimes I need to deny the memories, little one. I know you are in me. You are I. I hurt. I remember and I am 'Reace. I'm sorry that sometimes I need to separate. I'm doing my best. I don't always have to hurt. No, I don't always have to hurt."

Brushing my teeth again, when I remember these things my mouth feels dirty. I brush my teeth a lot.

June 3/89

Often now, I cannot remember what day it is. I believe I need a rest, a holiday. I'm looking forward to going to camp the first week in July. I've really frightened myself this time.

Receiving funding and taking the job as researcher and then being paid for it. Me? Yikes! No, I think I am finally seeing the reality of what I am doing, the possibilities and risks of falling on my face!!! What to do next?

What I am doing today, feeling powerful, is opening doors in my past that were powerfully terrifyingly abusive. That was a mouthful. (March, 2009: what a play, the feeling powerful thing. I did not feel powerful only vulnerable and very afraid. I was tricking myself in order to get something done.) I remember being inside of the coffin when I was little. It was quiet in there and dark. Just for a little while they said, you be real quiet and it'll be over real soon. We were at a graveyard, a place that little grandma was buried. The people in the dark robes were all there. The moon was big and bright.

Up until I began doing therapy I was always terrified of the full moon. I didn't know why then. I was just afraid. I guess about 3 years ago I stopped being afraid and began to see the beauty of the moon and the white magic. (Not really true because the full moon in March 2009, I became aware of this incredible anxiety inside of my body. I had a physical need to run and not stop running. I watched this feeling and felt it in me. Yuck, it was not a nice feeling. However, as I was at work all I could do was be aware of my feeling.) Today I love to stand in awe and wonder of her. Yet it wasn't so long ago that when the moon came to her fullness the people would get strange and their eyes would be all glassy. Another breakthrough, they were all high on drugs. They were stoned out of their trees.

So many moons, so many services. I got lost inside, my only reality was me and my dolls and my make-believe family. When I was 5, something terrible happened and we had to move up north and we stayed there for 3 years. My mom started to lose her hair when we were up there. She had lupus, the doctors said. I found this out when I was much older.

"There was this really pretty little lady and she was so nice to me. I thought she was going to help me and take me out of that room but she took me to the center and gave me to the big man. I screamed and screamed but they didn't care at all. He took my cloths off, there was a bowl of blood and he started to put it on my head. All the time he did this everyone made funny moaning noises. He put it all over my body. They said I was the devils' child and they were giving me to him. Then the man put me on the table and tied me there. The lady came and put a needle in my leg, Everything went far away after that."

June 4, 1989

I could see what was happening but I could not feel, as if I were watching them do those things to someone else. I began losing feeling in my body; today I know it is called multiple sclerosis. When I was 18, I started having symptoms and when I was 28, I was diagnosed as having M.S.

The mind is so powerful, so incredibly powerful. I needed to dissociate, to not be a part of my body's experience and that is exactly what my mind created for me to enable me to survive. "The little pieces that were on the table between my legs, I ate them because they were a part of me and they belonged inside of me".

The day that I relived this enactment was difficult. It was hard for me to own that I had eaten parts of myself, so very painful to remember this. When I did this, I remember being so very proud of myself, as if I put myself back together and they couldn't wreck me.

Children's minds are so fascinating.

I'm feeling so very disconnected and yet so very here: must be writing this story that is at least helping to create this experience for me. Either that or I am losing my mind! Today was full of earthy normal things for me. I spent time in my kitchen doing potato salad; I lay on the grass in the shade because the sun was so hot. I watched movies on television and I talked on the phone. Real normal everyday sort of stuff.

June 10/89

People don't want to hear what really happens. Not really hear. It's okay to read stuff in a book or a newspaper, but when I talk to people and I share little bits of my past, they get uncomfortable. So I put on a mask, or I just say things that they want to hear. But they can say anything and I listen. Well sometimes I get tired of being there for them and I change the subject. I guess that is a cop out because I could say I can't be here for you right now.

One woman I was having a long distance conversation with said, shut up so I can hear myself talk, I phone you so I can listen to myself talk. She did not hear herself say these words, but I did. I felt hurt. It's as if I am only a mirror to her, she can't see me. She doesn't even see me. I feel used, almost as if I'm helping her masturbate herself. So many people have ears and yet they do not use them because they don't really want to. So many people do things and they don't see what they are doing.

I get tired of coming out and being there for them and they can't be there for me, so I go inside for a while and it makes them mad. I don't care if they get mad anymore. I used to be afraid but that was because I couldn't take care of myself, now I can! Yahoo!!

Alan Watts's writings are what suits my mood these past days.

More and more I find myself unable to label anything. Things are and I just observe them. Some days I am out there in the play, playing. The play seems so real when I get into it.

When I was little, I was in the play. My mom and dad were lost in the play and I was a part of their play, for I had no choice when I was little. I remember one service they had. "There was a circle of people all dressed in dark robes and in the center of this circle there was a little girl. The little girl was I! We were all outside and it was dark and cold. There was a chicken and a kitty too. A big man I think who was in the middle too, yes it was a man and there was a lady too. They were saying weird things and holding the kitty and the chicken up high in the air. Then the man held the kitty out in front of him and cut the kitty's head off and the chicken's head too (They didn't bleed too much). He let the blood drip into a bowl that was on the ground in front of me".

It's as if I am watching this and seeing it like I'm watching a movie. Again, I need to say that this happened a long time ago. It is not now! The little girl watched this process with fear and bug eyed terror.

"Next the man put his hand on my left arm and held it tight. As if I could move!! He cupped some blood in his other hand and started to slowly put it on my body. I didn't have any clothes on and the blood was warm and sticky on me. The man made funny moaning noises when he was abusing me. There was no sound that would come out of me. The people in the circle were making humming noises while he did this and then he made me stand in the bowl and he started to cup the blood in both his hands and put it on my head."

It ran down my face and I started to cry like I am right now. Poor little girl with no one to help her make them stop.

"When he finished I got out. It was like I wasn't needed any more so I went over to the kitty and got her head and put it back where it was supposed to be but it wouldn't stay on. It kept falling off and I cried harder. The people started to laugh because they thought it was funny. Poor kitty, your head won't stay on. The chicken's head won't stay on either. I sat them beside each other and propped them up against the bowl and then put their heads on and then they rolled off so I held them in my arms and rocked them and I cried for them because I cared about them. I don't remember any more of that night, I think I went to sleep because I didn't want to be there any more."

This happened 35 years ago and I still feel the life force of the warm blood and finally it is safe enough to grieve for the little one who was subjected to these happenings, to grieve for me who was once this little one and to say, I'm so sorry that these things happened to me, that these things were done to me and to say, you truly are a wonder 'Reace to be here today. Thank you for being strong.

June 17, 1989

Some days have passed since I last wrote and so many things have happened. An article came out in the local paper last Wednesday about the second-stage housing society that I am developing, with the help of a steering committee. The day after, a big city newspaper contacts The National, a TV show and me. The Minister of National Health and Welfare was making a political statement and I was on the air because Health and Welfare Canada had funded the research project for the second-stage project we were working on. Yesterday I was interviewed and it will be aired for all of Canada to see. Lots of powerful things are happening for me in my now life!

June 22, 1989

I've found myself staying away from this room and yet tonight I am pulled in here. Tomorrow is Fathers Day and I have been desperately trying to pretend that it is not! That was all I had to write to get the tears flowing.

Why does it have to hurt so much? Pretend, pretend, and pretend. But it doesn't stop the hurt! I hate him, I hate him!!!

I remember hearing, "Be nice to Daddy. Just for a little while, it won't hurt, I promise it won't hurt."

"Daddy stop it, don't Daddy, Please Daddy don't, it hurts Daddy, you're hurting me, don't please".

"You know it's daddy's special day and you have to be good to me."

"Daddy, it hurts up in my tummy, I don't want it in my mouth, I don't like it".

"Yes dear, I know but it'll hurt more if I have to push it."

"Get it out! Get it out!!!!! I don't want it, I don't want it, I don't, I don't, I don't. You're hurting me".

Now I remember why I don't like Fathers Day.

A little later.

I had to stop typing for a bit. My throat has swelled up and my chest is full of pain, my throat and tongue are sore and I'm having a little trouble with my breathing. If I don't take it easy, I'll end up having a heart attack. Oh God! Ow. As I sit here typing through the tears and anguish I have become aware of, I'm sitting with my legs crossed very tight. No one will get in me.

Before I started to remember, I was living in oblivion. I had very little awareness and constantly put myself into situations where I was always being physically hurt and abused. I did the drug scene in my later teen years to help the oblivion happen faster. So much! Too much!

When I first entered therapy my question was, why do I think I deserve to be abused? And next was, why don't I deserve better?

The earth day is fathers day, June 18, 1989.

People put so much into the symbols that are only man made. After all it is really just another day. The sun is shining and there are white puffy clouds in the sky, the animals are out in the yard just like any other day.

This area that I have entered in my now life seems to be levelling out the teeter-totter. Being interviewed for national TV news seems to be an everyday normal experience that is really no big deal. Like it is all in a day's work. I'm still me, no different than the day before that, maybe a little more knowledgeable but that's all.

Not so very long ago, I would not have been able to cope with the pain of the memories that I am having. I would have had to be in a therapist's office where it was safe to remember and have my pain validated. Now I validate myself. The stronger I become out in the world, the more capable I am of handling the memories of my past. I'm OK, I'm really OK. I'm a survivor!

My studies have brought to my attention that a limited amount of information on ritual abuse is available and that there is a widespread discomfort felt by the public and professionals alike when considering the bizarre, aspects of "ritual abuse". I'm hoping that the readers of this information will become more aware of this reality. This is how I balance my pain, by wanting to help others in the world.

June 23, 1989

I feel quiet inside of me today. I can hear the wind chime that I made out of shells that were brought to me from the east coast. My fear had been getting control of me. I'd had the idea that my father just might come to my house today. I don't want him here! Strange that such a little man could have me so very afraid. He really is little. The ocean is calling me today, hearing the shells outside so I think I will drive to the beach today.

June 24, 1989

Another day, another time. The day's roll on and on, it's as if I am not connected to the days or the time. Seems strange that I would get so lost in what I am doing that I would lose track of time so very easy. There is so much to do in one lifetime. My days have been so very full with putting the second-stage transition house out into existence. The little part I did on The National was good. The next morning, a very powerful woman whom I admire, called me to say she'd seen me on The National and that I did good, she said. She also asked for my statistics about how many women and children had actually approached an 8 bed transition house and been turned away. I told her that 352 were turned away and she was taking this information with her for her case with the mayor. I was pleased. I felt totally validated.

I like it when I come back to this place inside of me, it's as if I am taking time out. There is one week left for me to get things in order so that I can take a week off and go to camp.

This is Saturday again, hard to believe. Both of my sons are up at their father's place tonight. They are having a barbecue my younger one tells me. Tomorrow I am taking the boys and a friend up to the water slides. My special friend, the one that also has a weird father, and her husband are coming with us. We will all have a picnic together. Seems like I am in another world when I am not out there working. I like this place.

For some strange reason, I feel like I am a cat that has swallowed a canary. Pleased with myself! It has been a month since I began writing this journal. Yes, I think I will call it a journal instead of a book. It will probably take a year to complete this project. There is no hurry, for what does it matter? Acceptance of self is why I am so very pleased. (Jan. 2009: and now I am... am what? Referring to publishing as a book? Its taken more than twenty years!)

My dreams are still unclear to me. There are many different dimensions of the self in my dreams. Peculiar, curious dreams they are. I dream of a multiple self, within myself. I dream of a self who can and does take charge and a self who is disconnected from the happenings of death and feeling. Today, parts of my body are numb; not quite all the feeling is present in me.

June 25, 1989

Last night I dreamed a woman was holding a very tiny baby. She looked like a woman I used to know. She dropped the baby; it started to roll down the hill. It was as if the woman was not conscious of this at all. I started to run after it but it was always one step ahead of me, I couldn't catch her. She went over the edge and landed in some water, and then she bounced up onto a ledge. I got to her and I picked her up. The life force left the infant's body. She was dead.

I took her back to her mother to give the mother her child. The mother seemed not really here, I grabbed the mother and shook her, yelling, this is your baby and she is dead. There was no effect. Another woman was there and I asked her what she thought? Was the woman a multiple personality and was there any sort of help for her? When I picked the baby up, I noticed she was all curled up in a little ball, like a small kitten. Almost as if it were an infant in a fetus stage yet to be born. I wonder if I am beginning to remember the miscarriage that I had when I was little.

I remember the summer that I bled for 32 days. My mom was thoroughly disgusted with me because she had to buy me a box of Kotex every day. I would go through 12 pads a day. About 2 years ago I remembered a large lump in the toilet bowl, which seemed to go with my bleeding for 32 days. Now I have this dream! My grownup self is aware that I did have a miscarriage.

When I gave birth to my second son, the doctor asked me how many abortions I'd had. I said none because "I" didn't. When I was 27 years old and had to have my uterus removed, the results were that the walls were abnormally thick with scar tissue. Again the doctor wanted to know how many D and C's I had. I said that I never had one, that I'd had 2 pregnancies and 2 baby boys because that is all that "I" ever had.

My grown self says that I must have had a miscarriage but!! I can see it in the toilet bowl. There is no connection. Isn't it interesting that at the same time I write the dream, I also begin writing about that happening a long time ago? It was the summer that I turned 14 years. I can see her. The little girl who was not, I can see her. Strange because I never knew she was ever really here.

The first step is to see from a distance and when it is safe enough I will go and sit inside of the little girl who sat on the toilet so very far away. I don't even know her. That girl that went through all of those experiences. I know she is I, but I don't feel.

I don't really remember like it really happened. Do I want to? Reclaiming through these writings is what I am doing.

The other night when I went to my steering committee, I for the first time handed the power of my second-stage transition house over to the committee. Now I am an employee and not the power center. I feel like I let her go. Is she ready? Is she strong enough to survive? Did I let her go too soon? All these questions I have in me. All these fears. I'm going to drive myself crazy. Do you think I'll find that little girl who was not allowed to be? Maybe in writing I will.

Last night I also dreamed that I was going to miss the plane that was taking me to camp. I dreamed that I wasn't even packed when the plane arrived.

June 30, 1989

On June 25, my Maria fish died. My Maria had lived with me for two weeks short of eight years. I knew Maria was dying for two weeks. Her tank is empty and I miss her. My younger son dug a hole under the willow tree and I wrapped her up in cellophane and put her in a little box, then we buried her.

I learned many things from my Maria fish. She taught me how to be still with the water, she taught me how to be quiet and patient as I waited for her to come and visit with me. I wish she didn't have to go. I miss her not being here for me. It's like I haven't let her go yet. I can see her in that empty tank.

Last night I dreamed that I was swimming on the dry land. It did not feel right to be doing this.

My animals have been my family. One of my cats had to be put to sleep a few months ago and now Maria has gone. My life is starting to fill up with humans but I still want my special family, the ones that keep me alive. I sense an end of a way of being is coming and I hurt. I feel little right now and I hurt. I feel alone and sad. Death is not easy for me to accept.

When I was little, my friends were the animals, I used to talk to them and play with them. I couldn't bring kids home but sometimes I would bring a friend home. My dad would always do something to them. I right now am that little girl that knew that Daddy who did those horrible things to all the little girls.

All of a sudden I know. And I'm not crying, I'm sort of confused. A part of me says, well of course he did that. I'm curious. Why aren't I surprised? Hell, I am in pain; my chest is thick with grief yet to be shed. I am in shock! That's all I can figure. My chest is burning.

Tomorrow I take my dog Thunder up to the kennel and then on Sunday I go off to camp and I am looking forward to having a week off from the professional world.

July 14

I've been to camp and back now. I feel rested and nourished. It is taking me some time to come back. I'm not quite sure what happened for me at camp, but I do know and feel validated deep down inside of me. I am more present so that means that I must have done integration. Not too sure what though, at this time. It will come to my awareness when the time is right. It is a good thing that I can trust my own process and listen to myself.

There has been much for me to do since my return. There are many proposals due right now. Yike!! The ones that needed to be completed are done.

When I was at camp, there was this one particular evening that I paired up with a woman completely different from myself. We went on a journey inside of ourselves and shared with the other person. I was little in my journey. I went to a large stream and sat in the middle of it. Then I began telling the story that I needed to tell from this place.

The story: Another part of me was a little girl who took care of the little girl that my father abused. For this me there was no knowledge of the abuse that had happened. This was okay because both little girls decided who was going to be responsible for what. I (the rescuer) would sit in the stream and let all of the ugly flow out and away. I loved her but I didn't want her to tell me nothing. She (the victim) would come to me at the stream so that I could wash her. In this stream I was one with the water and the wind and the animals. There was nothing else at all except the sun and the rain. And then she would have to go back out into that other world where the people would do mean things to her. (June 29, 2010: I've been seeing myself, the self-in –denial, in others like the boss who has the game-playing husband. She chooses not to see and makes excuses for him. She reflects the part of me that has been in denial all those years. Wow! Big one for me to get.)

I guess what I did at camp was find that center place and wash it clean. When I was done telling the story the woman that I was working with said to me, " you tell good stories". I don't think she realized that it was a true story.

July 15/89

Today I feel quiet and a little sad. I do not understand what is happening inside of me. There is this confusion and a feeling of emptiness in me. It feels like a part of myself is gone and I do not know where. I keep covering my mouth with my hands. As if to silence myself. It feels as if something inside of me has snapped or? The worlds are coming together and it makes me feel insane.

Yesterday I said that I couldn't hear, well the little girl that Daddy abused did not have a voice so I did not need to hear. Deaf and dumb I was. Maybe I washed a part of me away when I was in the stream at camp.

When I was little I would always be afraid of me going down the drain in the bathtub. When I got older my mom would remind me of this. There was so little of me, maybe that is why I was afraid. Trying to hang on to what was left. And then there was nothing, I disappeared. Gone into a world far inside of the body. Maybe I let go of or cleansed part of me...

I just had a phone call. Just amazing how I can arrive and be so very present when I have to be. There is more to me than meets the eye! I'm allowing a part of me to do the internal work on me and I have a part of me who keeps watch.

July 16/89

The weather is drizzly and dark. A day for dreaming and staying inside where it is warm and cozy. For the longest time I tried to make sense out of no sense.

A body cannot make some sense with something that has not got any.

The rains are coming harder and faster. They make me feel sleepy and dreamy. The heavens have opened up and are washing the earth. I don't think the earth will ever get clean. I don't think that I will ever get clean. Maybe after I let go of my body. But I already did that. Now I want to reclaim me. All of me! I'll just have to keep crying all of the old pains out and then maybe I will be clean.

July 19, 1989

Yesterday I went to the place where I had begun my therapy. I'd borrowed some books a long time ago and I went to return them. Bob, with whom I'd originally begun my journey into me, was there. It was hard for me to see him; he had lost weight, which did not help. I'd seen him larger before and this time he was just a man. My little girl was present for a little bit because she said to him, "look at me Teach, see what I've done". He said that my little girl was a wonderful part of me and he gave me a hug as I left.

I had not planned on staying at all and yet when he asked me to come in, I did. Almost as if I was being led by an unseen force. I found myself in a place inside of me that just responded. Trance and dreamlike I felt while I was there. He said he saw heaviness about me and maybe it was because I had come back to this place. I do believe he is correct. The pains and the sadness inside of me that I had unlocked as I did my work with him. It appears I've come full circle.

I began the deep work in his office and now I go back to officially end an era of my life. During my time with him, I had learned why I'd believed I deserved no better than the abuse I had been subjected to. This man had held me, rocked me and cared for me as I had journeyed into the past that I had blocked so effectively. Before I had been sad, but I did not know that I was.

This man, I love to the center of my being. I had not known this tenderness before. I had not realized before, just how deep I had let this man into my soul. He just came in. I allowed him to care for me. He told me that he often thinks of me. I did not risk asking him why. It was enough to hear him say that he does think of me. Remembering all of the hurts that I went through and he was there with me. I have mixed feelings for him. (March, 2009 and I still do the body work therapy with Bob)

Later

Do you ever wonder why you are here? I do. I work; I raise my younger son and watch my oldest from a distance. I watch people do the things that they do and I get into and do what I do. I always come back to this place and wonder why! Why am I here? I've probably spent the majority of my life in shock. Observing is what I do a lot. Isn't it nice that after all of these years, I can look at my life? I think this is positively the greatest!!! I can actually watch what I do and the other people in my life I can see. I get such a chuckle out of this. I don't have to get lost in life. I can live it, watch it, enjoy and relax into it (life). I'm finally making it OK for me to be in this place inside of me. I've sometimes felt as if I've been copping out by not getting lost into things. It's like a voice or a shadow has been hovering over me saying, "it's not really real."

Once I dreamed of me going for a walk along a path, there was someone guiding me. To my left there was a field full of dead bodies and I saw some little green sprouts growing. I remember wondering, through all the slime and death, still the little sprouts grow. I walked straight to the end. There was a garbage can there and inside at the bottom was a baby girl wrapped in dirty torn rags. I picked her up and turned. My guide was no longer with me. There were lots of death people around me and I knew I had to keep walking. There was a car waiting for me. I made it to the car with the baby girl in my arms, once inside of the car I took the filthy rags off her and snuggled her into my arms. She was I! The little one that had been dumped into a garbage can and left to die. I fooled them!!!! I'm alive. (Jan. 2009, I'd walked into the shadow of death and returned without fearing evil.)

July 22, 1989

My little sprouts will grow also. There is sadness in me this night. A loneliness that is large in me. People come and go, in and out of my life. As I continue to grow, some of my friends stop seeing me. Inside, I am still I. I'm more assertive, I say what is on my mind and take lots of risks. This is where I am. I miss the special friends that I have made during my healing time. They also have gone another way. Or maybe it is me who has gone another way?

I have mixed feelings, mixed emotions and a blurry spot in my right eye. So what is it that I do not want to see? The eastern philosophers way is to say that there is rage to see, through the right eye. I am angry! Angry and bored and pissed off! I'm hurt and I feel rejected. Accepting that I can't have everything that I want and that I can't do everything, is hard for me.

I bought some flowers the other day and a new outfit. I suppose I'm letting me know that someone loves me, even if it's me. I'm tired.

Good night 'Reace.

July 25/89

Yesterday I stayed out in the sun for too long. Today I've had sunstroke and my back and legs are burned so that it hurts to sit or walk. I've been dizzy and sick to my stomach all day. So why did I need to burn myself? Maybe I turned the anger that I have inward.

The heaviness in me that was seen is frustration. On Sunday, I drove up to my friend's house and on the way, I actually thought about stopping by to say hello and look at my father of origin. Now I can feel tones of frustration. What I'd really like to do is scream at him. I'd like to pound on him and pound. He still pretends that nothing ever happened, maybe this is what I am working toward, a confrontation. There had to be another way for me to handle this. To approach him would be of no value to me. He would pretend not to know what I was talking or yelling about.

When the incest first came out just after my mother died, he said things like, I remember the boy next door doing something to you and I told your mother this. She said things like this always happen and not to make a big fuss over such a little thing. The funny thing is, I never said my father had sexually abused me. I just said I'd been remembering that I was sexually abused as a child. And he took it from there.

July 30, 1989

The days go by so fast. Sometimes I wonder if I'm really here. My body is remembering again. I suppose my body is always remembering, it is subtler at times, but right now it is strong for me. Last night I was woken with this incredible pain in my chest. I feel as if a knife has been inserted into my right breast. The pain was so incredibly intense in the night and throughout this day. I've been breathing into the pain in the hopes that the intensity will subside. I feel as if I have pleurisy in my chest.

Yesterday was the annual family picnic with some very special friends of the boys and mine. These are the people (family) who, when I left my abusive marriage, my sons and I moved in with for 3 months. My adoptive family. This home is where I began to begin my life. Anyway, at the party there were many little girls with dolls. I found myself watching all the grownup women attend to these dolls. I thought this to be rather odd. My friend's son put a rag doll in my lap. I held it for a while and then set it aside. Just before I'd set it aside, my younger son came up and said, "So I see someone has come to visit with you." And then the pain came.

All day I have been breaking out in a hot sweat. I had flashes of a room full of dolls and a little girl. My shoulder feels as if it has been ripped out of my socket. My body is remembering and flashing something from a long time ago. I sometimes feel as if I am on the verge of losing consciousness. Like just before you pass out and all things seem to be a fog and nothing really affects you. Like a dream.

All that is real right now is my house and what is inside of it. My older son is connected to my yard and me. My younger son and his friend, because they are here. And everything else has disappeared.

August 1, 1989

The dolls were a reminder of all that was, when I was little. I made all of the grownups disappear and all that was left were the dolls. But the grownups were holding the dolls. This did not make sense, there were not supposed to be any grownups in the world. But they were there this time. So, I seem to have short circuited because I've integrated the grownups into the place that there weren't any.

I've had a nice day today. A quiet day. My work is getting stronger in the outer world. As well as in my inner world. Things all seem to be coming together. Inside and out.

August 26

With a crash things are coming together, I think they are coming together. My entire middle section of my body is numb. My breasts, my solar plexus center, my stomach, my back and my fingers. I did go and see my doctor this time.

"I think it is the multiple sclerosis", she said. Well, I know it is. I am angry that this is happening to me. I do not understand why this has happened. For a little over two weeks now I've been numb. The doctor says I'm probably having a reaction to something. Is it the dolls? I have a rotten cold. My head is all stuffed up, full of the grief that needs to be shed. There is fire in me, I have a fever. My hands want to make fists. Anger makes me hot inside, I know.

I've had another birthday and now I am 39 earth years in this body.

I did a trade with a client of mine. Free massages for his 22-foot motor home. My sons, one of their friends and I went on a trip.

It is not possible to set all of the many issues that we all have aside. We all ended up with a cold. I truly know that a camping trip is not a real holiday for mom.

While on our trip, I visited with a friend from college. She and I went out to the resort for my birthday dinner. It was beautiful sitting on the terrace over looking the lake. After dinner we went back to her parents home where she is staying right now. She sat me down and said for me to close my eyes. Next thing you know, out she comes singing happy birthday with a cake all lit up. I blew out the candles and missed a whole bunch. That was OK because she lit them all again for me. Then she pulls from behind her back, a doll. The doll is a dresser doll and she has makeup on and high heels. Something began happening inside of me and I started to cry. I don't know why I began crying. The doll, someone being so attentive to me, all I knew was I needed to be with my friend, the one that has a dad like mine. Someone from the other world, the world of not being dirty was being nice to me. This hurts; I hurt so much inside of me right now. I'd felt violated by her coming into this place inside of me.

The dolls, what do the dolls mean? There is a world out there. There are so many levels inside of me. Go beyond, go beyond. This birthday was hard for me. Before it came I was saying I don't want to have a birthday, I don't like birthdays. I hate them! I hate them! I only remember part of one when I was a girl. I went numb because I didn't want to feel my birthday. My friend, she knows that birthdays are not OK for me. The friend that has a dad like mine.

My throat is all choked right now and I need to cough something up. It was just before my fourteenth birthday that I miscarried that fetus into the toilet bowl. It's probably going to take me a couple of years to write my journal.

Something different...

We now have 6 transition homes full of second-stage women. Yahoo! Until our funding comes through, we are going to run an outreach program. It is all meant to be.

Every year when I was little, my mom would ask me what I wanted for Christmas and I would answer a doll. My mom would make a bit of fun around this but I was so blitzed out I did not take it in. As long as I had a doll, I was connected. It was as if having a doll gave me an identity. My one focus outside of my introverted world. The dolls were the only things that were real outside of me. The two worlds are coming together; this is why I am so confused.

Later

I lay on the bed and kicked and pounded with my fists for a while and then I fell asleep for an hour and a half. I phoned my younger son up at his dad's to see how he was feeling. He says he's feeling fine and that grandpa came to see them. His grandpa cannot take them to the PNE this year because he cannot walk very far and he needs to take lots of little rests. The boys both received $30.00 to go to the PNE by themselves. I find myself feeling sorry for my father. Strange! As I was lying on the bed kicking, I was saying out loud, I hate my father! And now there is compassion for this human being who was so sexually abusive towards me for all of those years. Why can't he own what he has done and say that he is sorry? He continues to play the game of I didn't do anything to my children and look at how cruel they are to me. My ex husband came down a few months ago to ask me to make my father feel better. What about me???? Everyone forgets that he hurt me; no they pretend that he did nothing to me. I even get caught in this trap - making daddy okay.

What about me? It is taking everything inside of me to not go and wrap him in my arms as if he were a little child and tell him that it is OK. It is not OK to do these things to me or anyone else. I'm sorry you're hurting daddy but I am too. I can't, no that's not true because I could set me aside, I won't set me aside. I won't let myself set me aside no matter how hard this is for me. When I was little I learned well how to set me aside. It was easy. I was the little girl who was not allowed to be. It was easy. I wasn't here! There was no me!!!

I hurt, I hurt! Why is there no one to ever hold me? To say it is all right for me to be here and that I don't have to set me aside to make it all right for them?

I say it is OK not to run out there and fix him. I want to get strong in this place. All of those tapes about how selfish I am by not fixing and making daddy better; I want them to leave my mind and my body now! I need to stop writing. I need to leave this place in me. I love you 'Reace! I love you.

August 28

I'm still numb. I wonder sometimes, if I'm going around in circles! I know my father is not asking me to make it OK for him. It's all of the old tapes inside of my head. What would happen if I let him be responsible for everything that he did? I have this feeling that I have been being responsible for his wrongs, that he is the victim. Is this my way of keeping me from being the victim? As long as I can hold power. He had always made out that he was the poor daddy who needed to be pampered. He played victim as he abused me. This makes my head feel confused. If he was the victim and the abuser, what was I? Again I have this sense of helping someone masturbate his or her own sick need. I have a feeling of separating a part of me from his need.

I'll put him inside of a bubble and watch him from afar. That makes him separate from me.

I think I just made me not a victim with him.

September 12

Hello. I'm in and out of a time warp. The past is coming into the future, into the now. I cannot run any more. My fingertips are numb and raw. They feel as if the skin has been removed. I find myself wondering if the writings that I am writing are making any sense at all. I spent this morning crying. It has been some time since I last cried. It is time for me to let go of the abuse.

Today is the 6-year mark. 6 years ago today my ex-husband beat me for the last time. I could feel my head being smashed onto the ground and hear him yelling, "don't you know how much I love you, you fucking bitch".

I went numb as I almost lost consciousness. This is love? I got up off the ground after he had finished being spread legged on top of me so I could not get away. He had screamed, "Come out of there and meet me". I could not, would not meet a man like this. He never really got to meet me. I can understand his anger and his frustration but this does not make it all right to beat me. *I looked deep into his left eye and touched him and then he threw me yelling "you're not worth it".*

I walked into the house and began to unload the dishwasher, (something that felt normal to me) as I was doing this he was emptying my purse. He threw a ten-dollar bill at me and said that it was worth more than I was. I took the money and my bag and started walking out towards my car. He opened the hood and took out something so I could not drive. He would not let me have the car or the truck. I felt trapped when he blocked the driveway.

I began to walk. I never said a word; I just walked away and up the street. His dog was following me and I encouraged this. Him and his precious dog. I talked to the dog and kept walking as his truck came racing up the street. I though he was going to finish me off by ramming the truck into me. All he was concerned about was his dog. Why should I be surprised? First came his dog, then his man friend, then his sons; no first came his dope, then the others and maybe me, maybe!

A little later

My eyes are burning and I need to cry some more. My body temperature is up to where I am sweating. There is a fire inside of me, a raging fire. Tonight I am going swimming and I need this. Endings and more endings, always endings.

I finally phoned this man who had led me to believe that we might have a relationship, a friendship maybe, anyway he wasn't there so I left him a message on his machine that said: Hi, this is 'Reace, maybe this will get you out of my system. I'm feeling hurt and I'm feeling really angry and I feel rejected, yes maybe this will finally get you out of my system.

A teacher of mine he was for 2 years, he was attracted to me and did not lay clear boundaries with me and I think he has copped out of being up front with me. I really would have thought that he would have had more in him. He teaches all of these things and charges lots of money and he does not practice his own voice. I feel cheated and ripped off! Let it go! I want to shake him and yell at him. He plays at being GOD and then he acts like an asshole.

Sept. 13

I went swimming last night and I did my one half mile. It helps to move anger out of a body. I've been angry with me, allowing myself to give away so much of my energy! Not wanting to let go of my dreams.

The dreams that I dream in the night when I'm sleeping are strong. Me driving up a hill that is so incredibly steep. It is difficult to travel up this hill. It is really steep. A couple of times I cannot move forward and I slip backward. But that's OK, for me in the dream; I get back into gear and move forward again and again until I near the top. I've been climbing feet first and my body leaning back. Near the top I cannot do this, so I fall forward and grab onto the earth with my hands. I pull myself to the top and over the edge. I feel a feeling of great accomplishment. Next the hill is downward. I begin to travel down but I'm moving too fast because I run smack into the traveler that is in front of me. I then apply my brakes; I had to fall into the start. It was like jumping off of a cliff or the start of a roller coaster. I just had to trust that the universe would absorb me as a part of the whole. The traveler who I bumped into could take care of himself.

A long time ago I dreamed a dream that was similar. In this dream the man that I'm angry with was there. I, at that time could not make it up the steep hill. I had asked him if I could have a lift, he opened his car door and let me in to give me a ride up the hard part. I'd told him I did not have enough power in my car and he had front wheel drive. This time I made the climb by myself! When I had started the climb I had been in a motor home that was full and heavy, but by the time I neared the top the motor home was gone and I was on my own in only my body.

There is only me left! I'm feeling spacey today. I find it takes work to focus on something outside of putting my thoughts down on paper. A human phrase for this might be, gosh, you're really thoughtful today. I've had quite a time putting surface words and phrases to the feelings that I feel and experience.

Someone might actually think that I am not of this earth. I'm a visitor. My chest is full of a burning pain. There is a fire inside.

I've been following the soap opera called All My Children, and a scenario that they are using. Dixie is locked up and being convinced that she is going to hurt her baby so she committed herself. Well, it is pushing all of my buttons! She is in a room now and cannot communicate with anyone because she really believes that she is dangerous and of course she is gentle and would never hurt anyone. At first I could not figure out why it was making me so angry. I had been convinced for a long time that I had done something so terrible when I was a little girl. I stayed locked up and away from everyone so I would not hurt them. I find me getting angry with her for believing him. How could she be so stupid? How could I have been so stupid? I was always confused. People saying that I must have done things and me not remembering doing anything. My father had convinced me that I had been responsible for the mutilations that the cult had committed.

A woman I met a while ago tried to do that to me. She said that she had given me the office key and I knew she didn't. She started to yell at me and I remember being mad at her. My son was with me so I kept my focus on him and said let's go and we walked out. She was so incredibly angry with me. In the night I woke feeling really afraid of her coming in to get me. I even phoned her place and her husband said, "I would think that you would have nightmares after the way you acted when you were here."

I asked my son what he had seen and he saw what I just shared which was fairly straightforward. I ended this relationship after more crazy making stuff. It was like she always wanted to fight and I did not want to. She got fired from her job for similar stuff; I began to feel like I wasn't so off the wall.

Since then I was able to end the so-called friendship where I always listened. Anyway, I got me into that one. Sort of like a replay of when I was little huh? It took me a long time to get her out of my system and I still sometimes remember some of the little bits of good stuff, which kept me confused. She was like my mother. I'm angry with my mom for believing my father's lies. Maybe this crazy soap opera is going to assist me in making a very major break through. Sometimes when I work so hard to try and undo the confusion inside of me head, I get a major headache and then I feel really messed up. So I'm going to take a break for now. Who knows where I'll be next time.

October 8, 1989

Last week I went to see Bob, the man that I'd done therapy with for 2.5 years. My hands have been numb since July sometime and I had needed to find out why I felt like there was blood on them. Why I can't reach out and take some life for me. I remembered being in that ritual with the cat and the chicken. There was more. I had to put my hands inside of the dog's body. They said that I was responsible for the dog being ripped open. I did not want to put my hands inside. Two men took my arms and pushed them inside of the dog. I pulled some of his insides out in my hands and I held my arms high up in the air and I did what was wanted of me. I was one of them. There was someone holding my left leg so that I could not move. I was the center of the ceremony. They said that I was one of them. So I stopped being who I am and locked myself inside so that I would never hurt anyone again. My hands are remembering and my hands hurt, I am hurting now.

"I didn't want to do it! I didn't!"

You're not dirty little one. You had to do what they made you do. You would have been punished far worse if you hadn't done it.

"Poor doggy! I didn't kill you! You were already dead. It was warm inside of your body".

I remember what it felt like to feel the inside of the dog, the warmth that was there. I went crazy that night. I can feel her pain now because she is in me again, I am her.

I want my hands back. They are not destroyers and they are clean. You weren't dirty doggy. No you weren't. They said awful things about you and me. It was they, not us little dog.

So many tears I cry for you and me. There is no one else to cry for us. I'm all alone in my pain.

To relive and feel after all of these years is difficult for me. When I remember these things, I'm feeling and reclaiming a part of myself that I'd had to leave behind. The emotion tears at my chest and throat.

I'm incredible, I really am. Day after tomorrow I am off to a national conference in Montreal on Urban Safety and Crime Prevention. When the pain becomes too much to bare, I shift into a safer place and that place is my work. An internal protective response.

I received a note from my father. Response to my Father's Letter

November 18, 1989

Brian,
Am questioning as to why I'm finding the need to respond to your letter. I have this memory back inside of me. It is memory of a lifetime ago. Impasse, you say. Dead end, yes we have reached a dead end. The young girl that once lived in a part of your life, is no longer. I've included a copy of the latest news article about me, for your information along with one of my business cards.

My life is full of truths and memories of what was. I speak only from a place of "I" statements and have in my personal life only those persons whom are willing to speak from truth. I remember a life full of falseness, not so long ago. I suppose I am speaking in riddles. What I am saying is that "I" will hear those words that are spoken from a place inside of one, words of ownership and I statements. I only allow those who own their own histories to come into my personal life.

It would not be ethical for me to enter into a counselling arrangement with you. I hear your need to talk of the woman who was once my mother. I would out of caring for all human beings, like to refer you to someone. There are many professional persons who would be willing to assist you in processing your grief. It would not be fair for you to ask someone so close to the issue at hand to discuss the pain mother suffered.

Much work on myself have I done, to be able to cross past my pain of the memories of the assaults on my physical person to get to the place of being able to write these words down on paper to you. I suppose I am giving the small person inside of me, a gift. To be able to step beyond is quite an accomplishment.

What I am asking of you is, that you bring the truth forward. I do remember what was. None else will I receive? And if you do, I know that I will again be in pain, but it will be the pain of release. A healing will take place for all. It is hard for me to write these words.

None else will I receive?
Sincerely,
'Reace

December 2, 1989

Seems like a very long time ago since I've written in this journal. The days and the months go by and I am not aware of the speed.

It seems that I live in a world that is made up of seasons. Well it is, isn't it?

After reading my father's reply to the letter that I had responded with, I feel it is over. All of the hopes that I'd ever had of him owning or saying that he is sorry, are over. And the funny thing is, he was never accused of anything. On the day my mother died, I had said that I had found out, remembered that I had been sexually abused as a child. He took it from there.

I hope that I do finish and publish this journal before he is dead. I need to have a private ceremony of the death of an illusion, of the death of any hopes that I had around a happy-ever-after-ending. The only happy ending is that 'Reace sees the light and holds her head up and moves ahead into her own future. There is a sense of relief in me. Also a sense of his ugliness is about and I need to clear it out of my space.

I sound more and more like a counsellor every day.

My trip to Montreal was fabulous and highly educational. Very exciting also. There were over 900 delegates and 31 countries that attended and I was one of them. Is it OK for someone who is going political to have a background such as mine? Wow, wouldn't the press have a riot with this kind of muck? So what do I do? I'm not ever going to pretend that my life was not. It was my life experiences that made me the woman that I am today. That song that goes, I'm coming out, is going through me right now.

My ankle where it was held tight so long ago is numb. I still have some numbness is my trunk, my hands and legs. The energy is not flowing through me clearly yet. So maybe I again need to do some work with Bob? Twice now I've been back. Just after I returned from Montreal I was in to see him. I integrated a part of me that I had sent away over a year ago. A part that comes out too far, a part of me that I was afraid of, I reclaimed this part of me and I cried as I embraced myself.

December 8, 1989

For some reason I'm here, in my office at 11:04 PM. I'm not quite sure why I need to be here. But here I am, at my typewriter. This morning I felt full and loved. I put on my white sweater dress and went off to my practicum. When I had spent the 3 years being taught by Martin, he had liked me in my white dress and I had felt appreciated by him. I had felt womanly and attractive. The day before, a woman had shared with me that Martin had passed on a hello to me. This made me feel cared for. He really had been a strong influence in my life. I've missed him this past almost 2 years.

So many feelings in me. When I stop to think, I hurt inside. No wonder I work so hard. My strong focus on my outside work keeps the inside not being touched. And then the pain gets so unbearable my body reacts by having Multiple Sclerosis symptoms. I talked to my brother this evening. He said I had put his thoughts into words. But they are my thoughts because I wrote them.

I need to sit in my stream and let myself be washed. It is so very quiet in my home this moment. Today had been a busy day for me. I am tired.

Dec. 9

This day has been weird. Really weird. The sky is clear and bright. The stars sparkle beautifully and I have a wonderful calmness in me. My day began with a friend calling me to come and give her a massage. She has a lot of bitterness inside of her and she was quite verbally abusive to me. Yet I went down and saw her. It is her stuff and I don't want to take it on. She proceeded to assume things and phrases for me. I found it interesting how she was able to carry on a conversation with just her. She would talk for both herself and me. How she ever figured that she knew what I was thinking amazed me.

My special friend, Jerry is returning home tomorrow. I hope that she is well. We have not been seeing that much of each other lately. We've both needed to work a great deal of the time. I'm in my space inside of me and I like being inside of me. Quiet in me.

I feel as if I am in a world that is protected from the abuse of others and I feel warm and wonderful. It's as if I have a magic man in my life again. I do. He is returning into my life and I welcome him with love and tons of warm fuzzies.

Today I went grocery shopping and then I did a little bit of Christmas shopping. I also got Roy a birthday gift. On the 17th my baby turns 15 years. I bought him a nice card and now I can't find it. Maybe it will turn up.

Last night I had said that I needed to go and sit in my stream and wash. Well I do believe that I am there, here. Time out. I wish he, my magic man, would come and visit with me. I've missed him so much. When I talk about my magic man, well, this visit would be a magic visit. Some children create special friends to keep them company when they are small. Well to survive, I've had to have magic friends all of my life.

Dec. 10, 1989

The weather was simply marvellous this day. I baked shortbread cookies this morning. I made 6 dozen of them. Next I went off to collect both of my boys. Roy's friend came along also. We went out to a tree farm and chopped down our Christmas tree. We ended up with 2 trees. One big one for the front room and one little one for Roy's room. John came down for dinner and he helped to put up the tree. Our house looks and feels warm. John got real quiet today. He seems to have some heavy thoughts to tend to. Too many for such a young man. My older son has chosen a difficult path to follow. It is his path and I must respect this for him.

All of a sudden I have acquired this patience. Very unusual for me. I'm not getting lost in other's issues. Strange. What I should be working on is my information that is to go on a report for this meeting. I figure I'll have some time early in the evening of the 12th. Just in time too. The meeting is on the 14th.

To read the different thoughts that I put down on paper is a strange feeling for me. There are so many different thoughts that I have. I'm always questioning myself as to whether or not I am a sane person. Because a lot of the time I feel not so sane. I bet a lot of persons don't even think about it. Maybe it is just because I am reaching my 40th year. Time to reflect on where I've been and wondering just where I am going to end up. So many worlds I've already lived in, no wonder I am losing my mind. The things that I have seen and felt.

Dec. 16, 1989

A few times I've had input for this journal, yet I did not come in and sit here to type. Tomorrow my younger son turns 15 years old. Where is yesterday?

I wanted to write down a dream I had since I last wrote in you. This was a dream at the full moon. I was traveling with two others and I was the one that did the talking. At first I was driving a car. We came to a winding road and yet I knew this road well. I swung out to the left and then there were a lot of curves in the dirt road. There was maintenance being done on the road along the way. It had been a long time since I'd last traveled this road. All of a sudden I was walking in a glen. There were trees all around us. One of the women that I was traveling with stopped and sat down. I continued with the other woman. I looked up and there was a clearing. What I saw were ships parked up where the clouds usually are. Many different sized ships. I asked the woman beside me to look up and see. She looked up but did not see the ships. What we both saw was a bird, the bird was prehistoric. A very big bird that had a large beak and a huge wingspan. It was flying high in the sky. All of a sudden a bird from below flies straight up and opens it's beak and clutches on to the large prehistoric bird. It flies back down with it in its beak.

A most interesting dream. I felt as if I were traveling through time. The very distant past and future. Or really seeing what there is right now if I only take the time to look.

Tonight I become aware that life and death are thoughts that we create. I feel as though I'm in a time warp. A place where things are. The earth realm is only a very small part of what there is. There is so very much more for us to see and learn. I own that. There is so very much for me to see and learn. I feel as if I have shut down the outside world for a little while. It becomes overwhelming and overloading for me. I like to take time out inside of me. I'm beginning to forget things. It does not seem as important for me to remember everything anymore. I take notes so I know what I need to do tomorrow.

There are new people in my world. I seem to be making friends on a different level. Some of these people I will keep my eyes open with. There seem to be many hidden agendas with some. I find it strange that people would find it necessary to have a hidden agenda with me. Whatever do they perceive with me? This is definitely interesting.

Dec. 17

I'm feeling some sadness today. I feel so isolated with all that I carry within me. What am I meant to do with all that I have learned from my experiences? Add them to who I am. Pretend to play the game called life. I feel removed from life experiences and in a world of my own. Do we all experience these feelings? Some may say that I'm crazy. Sometimes I think that I am crazy. I'm afraid to get back into life. I do not want to lose me again.

The tears well in my eyes. This is obviously truth for me. I stand on the edge. Yet I can get into things when I feel the need. I feel as if

I am watching. Yet I know this is not always so. Maybe I should enjoy where I am. From this place I can be aware. So what am I worried about? All a part of growing up. My younger son is 15 today.

Today I go to the alderman Open House. I've definitely entered a different play. There are so many worlds to visit in this one life. People are neat. I like a lot of them. The women who are in my now life are great. They're a lot of fun, too. All women who are going out into the world filling their own needs. Growing and exploring what there is out there in the world for all of us. I enjoy this.

There are too many stop signs in the world. There are too many saying that we must not do. I say, why not? We have all been given a life to live. What does it matter what body we are in? All I do is say what should be for all and I get told that I should be in politics. This is strange. We were all born as human beings. We should all do what we need to do. I'll add that it is OK as long as we do not violate another beings space or destroy, destruct, we have a right to live.

Later

Why do I feel as if I would like to thrust my arms out and wipe my slate clean and begin again? I want to get rid of all the garbage and start again. Get rid of?? Yes, this is what I am feeling. The adult in me is angered. Angered with my father of origin. The denial that he offers. I am outraged. I have tucked the little one inside of me, tucked her in safe from the energy that he offers in this direction. A mother bear I am. Mother to myself. He is the garbage that I wish to get rid of. I walk around for such a long time before I realize what is happening inside of me. As a mother who has had her small daughter raped by a full-grown man, I wish to kill. I know I would not in the physical world but I need to end his life inside of me. The pain in me is so strong. I hate him for what he has done to me.

He took away so much of my life when he raped me. They had to sew me up because he ripped me open. I was only a babe. I was three years old the first time he penetrated me. And he denies that he did anything to be ashamed of. I will not let him touch my little one ever again. I see him sitting on the planet and I take my hands and arms and fling them out completely cleaning the planet of his being. I want him dead.

I lost 34 years of my life because of what he did to me. For 19 years he used me and pretended that he didn't. He fucked my very mind with all of the lies he told. He said what was happening was not really happening. I need to get rid of him from me. Maybe I should stab a pillow until I am so tired I cannot move. Then throw the pillow out in the garbage. He threw me in the garbage can when I was a little tiny girl. I've had to wash and wash to clean myself from all of his sperm and mucus. He put it on my whole body. I guess he thought he was an animal who needed to mark his territory. My mouth is full of phlegm. That needs to be spit out. The vile disgusting past that I was made to live in.

And the weirdest part of all is: I still have not accused him of anything. All I ever said was that I'd remembered being sexually abused as a child. I have said none else to him. Outside of the letter that I just recently wrote to him. I talked to my friend B.A. and she listened to me and heard my pain. I'm glad she called. She is offering to give me an old pillow to kill. She also suggests that I maybe go and do some more work with Bob. Good idea. Having one's pain validated helps to make everything so real. I will clear my father out of my psyche.

December 25, 1989

Christmas day and here I am. I feel like I need to escape. More and more I feel the need to leave this planet behind me. The pain that I feel as I stay. Does not matter what I do, I still cannot get away from the pain and loneliness that I feel. Both of my sons were here last eve. I wanted to wrap them both up in my arms. They have their boundaries so I did not. I am frustrated and fed up. Is this the way I must spend the rest of my earth life? I've gone to a different level in my work with my clients. To do this I have taken a very big risk. I'm not sure if I want to continue. I get so fed up with the small minds of man/woman. I am tired. I seem to be spending the majority of my time being fed up and tired.

So why do I not make this life different for myself? You would think that with the powers and knowledge that I have in me, that I would change things for myself.

Does everyone who has been violated the way that I have, feel as I do? Lost and hurt and always needing to cry. I want this pain to go away. It is messing up my life. People that are near me are more in touch with their pain and sorrows. My words are more profound than others, says my college instructor. And he likes this. I feel as if I have been cursed. It is hard to live truth. It is easier to pretend and lie. There is at least a lot more people to communicate with. So many lies are told about how one feels because it would make one too vulnerable to tell. Maybe I'm having a nervous breakdown. Maybe I am just due a good cry.

Did I ever write down about the bodies all over the snow? The ones that were all cut up and red blood was everywhere on the white snow? Every winter I start to get afraid. I do not like to go out in the car in the winter. I like to walk and stay near my home. It is safer that way.

I just looked up the word profound and it means very learned, deep. I have always been a very sad person. I remember when I was much younger; I would lie on my bed and cry and cry. It used to drive my mother crazy. Once they had my Aunt visit and try and straighten me out. She said that I was fine. What did she know?

The amnesia is starting to come back again. This makes me very concerned. I blank out sometimes. I forget who I am for a moment. I woke the other night feeling all turned around and not knowing where I was. I remember thinking, it is happening again.

Feeling disoriented, confused. Why after all this time is this starting up again?

It's the pieces of bodies and the blood. They would go and find little children and they would hurt them. After the ritual there would be pieces left over.

When I was 16 or 17 I would have these funny passing out spells. When I was 28 they thought I had petit mal seizures. But what I really feel is the confusion. I told Jerry last eve and she said that it is what a multiple feels. But I am just me all of the time. There is a part of me that is still missing. The part that went to elementary school has not come back to me. I know this because I cannot remember anything about school at all until some things in high school. Who is she and where is she? Why don't I know her? I would like to meet her.

The change would happen as I went through the gully on my way to school. I was not a very bright child. I was not that present. There was a lot of fuzziness for me. I can't remember going to school up on the mountain when we lived up North. We were there for 3 years.

Later

I'm feeling better than I was earlier. I had a nap on the chesterfield. I watched a really cute movie on pay TV. I had some dinner and now I'm feeling not too bad. I was wondering if this journal makes any sense at all. I wonder this often and I've probably already mentioned this. As I was writing earlier I had a sense that the part of me, who I do not know, was beginning to come out and write. I started to recall some visual pictures inside of my head. Most of the time when I am writing I am crying. This is why I stay away from my journal so often. This is also why it will take years to complete this.

Time does not mean so much any more anyway. The lines on my face are really apparent now, so this is why I do know that the years are going by. The seasons change so quickly now. I need to go to the Island for a time. It has been almost 2 years since I was

Reace

last there. Maybe when I've completed my practicum I might have a little time to go.

I do not like to have my brother know all of what my needs are. Weird eh? Because one day he will read my journal. Maybe so. It will bring him much pain. After all he was very much a part of the abusive world that I once lived in. He was there as a silent witness. And sometimes abused as well. He got to see and he does not like what he saw. I feel like an intruder in anyone's life if I ask for something. Always looking to fill their needs. It is hard to fill mine.

Dec. 26,1989

Very soon it will be 1990. I spent time visiting friends today. Special friends came down to visit this morning. They had put me up when I left the abusive relationship I'd been in with my ex-husband. They will always be friends of mine. It was at their home that my second stage began. This is where I began creating the second-stage transition house for battered women and their children.

I'm feeling more grounded tonight than I was yesterday. I need to feel solid and in my own power. Otherwise I feel as if I am going insane. That is when I begin to lose touch with the reality of the earth realm. It is like the land of fairy.

I can come back to this place by talking to a colleague. B.A. just called me. I like to talk with her. She is fairly solid and grounded in the working world. Just what I need right now. I did need to leave the working world for a little while. It is nice that I can come back. I had been feeling a little frightened about going off the deep end. A not so nice place to be. Next time I decide to go there I need to set up an anchor in the working world for me. I guess that is why I'd been trying to get hold of B.A. for 3 days. It was safe for me to check out for those few days. I often wonder how my 2 sons experience me.

I went to Carrie's open house this afternoon for a little while. I like Carrie. I met her when we worked together on an article to stop some horrible news about my son being retarded. My son has had dyslexia and that does not make him retarded. It was cruel what had been written about him and some other children. Anyway, Carrie helped me give them what for. So that was the start of what would turn into a very close friendship. After all, she is now the president for the second-stage transition house. I feel OK having her in this position.

I'm going to go to bed now, good night 'Reace.

Dec. 27, 1989

Sometimes I want to hide inside and not come out at all. It is like I have to force me to get up and do. Today I could have stayed in bed all-day and just hibernated. Lots of folks feel like this some of the time. The boys and me are off for Christmas dinner with my brother's family. And I just want to curl up and stay cozy at my house. I know that once we get there we will have a nice visit, so I must pull on some energy and come out for the visit. Maybe I should just go in....sane for a while. Might be a nice break for a while. Time out is what I need. A long quiet holiday.

In 9 days, well 9 working days into the new year, I will complete my Community Social Service Worker program. Jan. 12, 1990 I will have my last working day as a student. I am very excited about this. Quite an accomplishment for me. What will I do next?? I get a kick out of watching where I will go next.

Soon I must go deep inside of me and remember the white snow that is covered in red blood. I know that the time is coming for me to do this for myself. Confront, face, grieve and accept so that I can move on in the world. Maybe this is why I am beginning to journey into me so deep. I am already nearing the place that I will be able to begin recalling that horrifying day.

Tomorrow I work over at the non-profit society that I am the developer for. I have two 1 and a half hour counselling sessions to facilitate. When I am in this place of pain and quiet, I work well for others. I am vulnerable and extremely sensitive.

It is time for me to gather the gifts and the goodies that I will take with me to my brother's.

Hi, I'm back. We had a nice dinner at my brother's home. The little ones were fun. They had lots of hugs for me.

I get home and there is an emergency at the second-stage complex. So I arrive quickly into my professional self to deal with the situation. I found me getting a little defensive of my concept for the women at second-stage. Interesting that I felt that I needed to defend me. I'm glad Lynn called me on it. Was neat because I have been validated. I get that I was not even being questioned. This is nice to be supported. I have much work to do tomorrow to get this one woman into a safer place. I feel strange inside of me. A little dizzy with this new feeling. Am nearing 40 years of age and I get to finally feel in me support by another human being. I think I will go to sleep now and let my dream handle this new input. Besides I do have to work tomorrow. I feel good to be writing again. Night 'Reace... You're going to be OK.

Dec. 28, 1989

For some reason I am angry, very angry and I do not know why. I have very little patience this morning. The anger is in me about something personal. What though? I am growling in my speech. I'm not directing my anger at anyone in particular. I'm just being angry. The people that I have talked to this morning are not comfortable with my being a grizzly bear. I am pushing my clients also. Questioning out loud their behaviour. Confronting when they back off of their commitment. I know I have high expectations of self and others. This is what I am told. I think what I have is the need for all to follow up on what they say. There is so much bullshit and phonies in this world.

I was phoney yesterday while I was at my brother's. I felt like I was in the wrong place at the wrong time. It was hard for me to be at his home. There are so many things that should be said and they are not. I am angry with my brother. He is in a fog. My grown self knows that this is his choice to stay in ignorance and shut out reality. Oh hell, whose reality? His is a world that I choose not to live in any more. I'm pissed off and have no patience to relate to that place any longer. It was me that could not be; no it was me who was not even seen yesterday. My expectations are that my brother would at least try to see who I am.

Since I have gotten in touch with what my rage is all about, I am feeling much clearer. Not so confused. Interesting, eh? I can see past my anger. I still need to talk to Lynn and thank her for not taking on any of my shit last night when we talked. I was a little rough on one of my clients and so I will own this with her. Hope that she is OK with the push that I gave her. Hell, maybe I should let her work it out for herself.

I was in the fog, the fog of my own anger. Pretending to not be who I am. It does not work any more. My client called me and rebooked her time with me. This is god working. She worked it out inside of herself. I enjoy assisting women in finding themselves. It is a wonderful feeling to give them permission to be and just do what they need to do and be okay with a little push now and then. Goddess I love it when I am feeling clearer and not so crowded in my own work. Yet I have a small blurry spot in my right eye. A part of my anger I am not seeing. So again, what is new?

January 21, 1990

I'm lost. Lost in time that moves too fast. I know that if I were to sit down and rethink the things that I have done in this last while I would be able to put things down on paper, but... I am too tired to make my brain do anything outside of wander to where it needs to go. I guess I am taking a day off. Yet there is a large part of me that would force myself to gather up some inside resource to enable me to function on a high level. I'm feeling the need to push everything out of my space right now. I do not want to work today.

My answering machine is on. I sit here typing and listen as the calls come in. Don't people know that it is Sunday? I am so tired of working seven days a week. I suppose it is up to me to set some limits for myself. If I do not set the limits I will soon burn out. I will have given me to everyone else. I find it ironic that these people see me as someone who knows. What the hell do I know? I have difficulty trying to get through my own life without coming to pieces. I am not comfortable being put in a place where I have the power to decide what happens in another's life. Have guidelines and follow them. Let the clients know that these are the guidelines and if they choose not to stay within the contract that they sign, they are responsible for the consequences.

I'm not so sure that I was made to be a leader. I always want to make things easier for people. But where would the world be if there were no rules to follow? It is hard to enforce the rules when you know that someone will hurt. But they hurt if you do not have guidelines. I do not like for people to follow me.... I wish for people to stand on their own feet. This is called transference, is it not? First they give to me their power and then I give it back. But I do not want it at all. I do not need power. It is not necessary to have this. It weighs me down. Yuck. I am heavy enough as it is. Carrying all of my own life experiences is more than enough thank you.

It is so hard to find space for me amongst all of the muck. There is so much outside interference in the world it is hard to find a small space to come out and breathe in. As I type these words that I am typing now, I have a sense that there is a very small part of me struggling to get her head above the water. I have been drowning in here. This little one whom I so desperately want to have the opportunity to be, is buried alive amongst the muck.

Seems that all I've been doing in the earth realm are, attending to everyone else's needs and not my own. Goddess forbid that I would actually want to be selfish and only think of me. Well, I do. At first I felt as if I needed to crawl inside of my old cocoon and curl up for a few hundred years of rest. This does sound tempting though. I am getting inside of a cave and curling up for awhile. Yes, this sounds and feels nice. A retreat would be nice. Let the world wait until tomorrow. I am not in time anyway, so what does it matter?

My young son is off on his snowboard this day. He is quite good at sports. I hope that he and his friends are having a good time. Always when I have found the outside world a bit too much, I have gone into this place inside of me to take time out. There is an earth realm, a land of fairy and a place to take time out. Kind of like the place called Avalon. This is a nice place.

A little while ago my body again was breaking out in bruises. They just pop out for no obvious reason. My right ankle always seems to be the color green.

The end of last week I had my final evaluation with my collage supervisor. I am now a graduate of the Community Social Service Worker program. He said, in the things that I am doing out in the world I am about 5 years ahead of my time. He is a little concerned for me, he says, because I will not have the supervision and the help of colleagues that he thinks would be good for me right now. I will search for a support system for myself. He also suggested that I find a safe man to continue my personal work with. This love hate relationship that I seem to have with men who are authority figures. I feel confused by the things he shared with me.

Again someone outside of me is telling me who I am. What I feel and what I need to do with my life. Always these things give me insecurities in myself. I am frowning right now with concern. Why did he need to say these things to me? And why did he say that preferably I should do my work with him? And then he adds that he is not available. These are all of the things that he said to me and I think they are his issues? I do not know anymore. A voice says in me.... Yes you do. Well, maybe I do somewhere know but I'm too tired to look, so there.

Jan. 27, 1990

Another day to play. I have had today off and I am feeling lost inside of me. I get tomorrow off as well. Roy is staying over at a friends house tonight and then in the early morning they are all going snow boarding. He will have fun. Roy is becoming a very good snow boarder. He says he needs lots of work though.

This afternoon I bought a DE humidifier for my house. Already it is getting warmer is this home of mine. Lots of water in this house. You know, I might actually learn to type if I continue to talk to myself on paper. Someone might think that I am a little bit of a nut case if they were to listen in on my thoughts some time. There seems to be a fair bit on the television as of late, on vampires and the occult. I watch and see parts of my past coming out at me in these shows. I remember the outfits that were worn. There is not as much fear in me as there was in the beginning of my remembering. After all it did happen a very long time ago for me. Gruesome murders on the television shows. Weirdo's writing in blood. (March 28, 2009. And I could see it was outside of me and on the television as well.)

Jan. 28

The storms outside have been strong all day today. I feel as if I am in again another world. Not being touched by the outside. I slept for a while and dreamed this afternoon. My father of origin was there in my dream for a few moments. Long enough to be busy telling my son to not let his mother drive the car. I walked up to him and said it was time for him to hear my perception of what I thought. All my life I had stood patiently and listened to what he had to say and now he could shut up and hear my perception. I said to him that he was a miserable bastard. He began to talk and I said "no more". I just walked away from him. In one part of my dream there was an old woman who was not breathing properly, I was sitting with

54

her. I asked her whom she needed to see? She gave me 2 male names. I was a little confused in the dream because I had thought that another name was to be called. I went out and called the names that she had asked for.

I've been rethinking on who I'm to be out there in the world. I meet some women and their concerns are: who is who and who should I have or do lunch with? This reminds me of my mother. I rebelled when I was a teenager because of this attitude. A lah DE dah kind of attitude. It is so incredibly phoney. And me, I've been playing this game lately. Yuk. Yuk. Well, one good thing is I haven't gotten lost in the attitude. I can lose myself as I'm out in the world. I'm not someone great enough to be acknowledged by one woman. This has hurt my feelings. I will not give her the energy. I will grow greater than she could ever think to be because I will not lose sight of the people. She has become lost in her own needs and glories. This is a very big trap. And I almost slid into it.

I need to do some more work on me. I need to grow more. I am still very young. There is much for me to learn. Very much more to learn. Maybe this door is meant to close now, so yet another may open. Maybe it has only been a playground for me to learn in. Yes, to observe and learn and grow from my experience. Yet a powerful woman has suggested that I run for council. I do not think this is where I am to go. It has only been an education for me. One world within the many worlds that I have walked in. Where to next?

I try on lives like other people try on clothes. Where do I want to walk now? It is a gift for lack of any other word to describe what it is like to be able to see another's path. There are many of us on this planet who get to see. I do need to do some more work if I intend to grow some more. There are too many blocks inside of my head. These blocks are because my knowledge stops. Or I am not strong enough to go ahead now. Time to be in me to learn more. When I am in this place inside of me I feel spacey. Almost high and quite trance-like. Maybe I should meditate for a time. Yes, I can do this while I walk around. I am quite skilled in this area.

Soon my son will arrive home from his ski trip. I do hope he has had a marvellous time. I worry when he goes out into the world of forces. Yet this is the world that he walks in for now. I know that there is much for him to learn in this world. His tools for his future are what he is gathering now.

Feb. 10, 1990

There is this restlessness inside of me. I am having difficulty with this feeling. There is a part of me that wants to cry out. There is a part of me that wants to thrash around. The energy inside of me is blocked and I feel frustrated with me. I am bored with my life. Bored and so very lonely. Yet my life is so full of so many things to do. Some are telling me how proud they are of me. Yet there is this frown on my brow. So why do I frown? I do not know. My dreams are full of lovers. Men who hold me and comfort me. I need to go out and dance and be in a partner's arms. Into my space I let men who are 60 or 20. I do not let the ones who would be lovers for me into my space. Why? Can I not yet be safe? Do I forever have to dream a lover, a partner for me? I feel empty without a mate. I cannot go back, not ever. So here I am, alone. Work is no longer filling this pain in me.

I have friends who call and they ask me to come out with them. They are in a place that I once was. Not knowing how to heal their Multiple Sclerosis and looking to me. Will I ever get to share with the world how they might not need to have this dis/ease? But there is and are lessons to be learned in having a dis/ease. I could become a wealthy woman if I was able to get out there and share how. But are they able to hear? I wonder.

Some of my dreams are not of lovers. I am being taken to a room to be analyzed by my therapist and he brings in another man. This frightens me. I was curling up in this huge chair feeling very tired and small until they came into the room. I got up and went into a smaller room. I curled up in the corner very frightened. I remember saying out loud in my head, "why is this happening again"? When the man came to get me at the start, he took my hand and led me. I said to him that this made me feel very small. It was as if there was a grown me and then a very little me. There is something going on in my unconscious mind that I as of yet am not aware. There is more of me out here in the earth world.

Tomorrow I go to the city for a balancing treatment. This will be relaxing. I hope so anyway. More personal life is what I am after right now. I'm bored because all I've been doing is working. Who wouldn't be bored?

My friend, the one with a dad like mine, Jerry is her name. Well she is in the hospital again. She tried to kill herself again. She is a multiple personality person. There are some new ones in her. Ones who want to push me away. They want to frighten me so I will leave her alone. Why does she need to not have me? I know that I have become a part of her. I told her last weekend that I would give her the space she wanted. I am angry with her. Annoyed is a better word. For how I feel. She cannot get out of that old place. She cannot accept that it was and it is not now... I died and sometimes I feel sad for the part of me that is dead. He killed her. He killed hopes and dreams that all little girls have. What was, was real. He did all of those ugly things to me.

Interesting that my friend is a multiple person and I developed Multiple Sclerosis. Similar, yes? Multiple people, multiple nerves. I have this knowing in me that she will never come out like I have. I need to let this be OK. Then she can have her life and I mine. Strange that I need to write these things because I had thought that it did not matter any more. I thought that I had gone numb in this place. Guess not. (March 28, 2009. And then again, perhaps she will out grow me by far.)

Saying goodbye to so many of my lives. It seems that I am always saying goodbye. I move on and she does not. Will she let herself live? I do not know the answer to this. I'm not going numb, I'm going hard. Yet when she said to me that she would get a bigger pair of scissor if I didn't back off, I was frightened. I know that I am not physically strong enough to defend myself from her, so I will keep me safe and stay away for now. I will not risk my life for her. I doubt if she would expect me to either. There are nicer ways to tell a person to get lost. Threatening a person is illegal.

February 19, 1990

I've just reread my last entry. I get that a very angry little girl inside of me was writing that day.

Again my life is changing, always moving and being different seems to be me. There is a great deal of anxiety inside of me lately. Frustrations and needs of greater spaces. I feel as if I need to shed another skin. Could be the bodywork that I've begun again. Last Saturday I experienced a great wholeness when the Jin Shin Do work was completed. An incredibly wonderful feeling for me. So what is this frustration right now?

I've decided to include that I have found my way of healing, having had M.S. After reading some of Shirley MacLaine's story, I feel more OK with it being all right to share my process. Thank you Shirley.

Being that little girl who was not allowed to be has taught me much. As a grownup person would take a part of me or abuse me, I would have my own special way of not feeling it. I would disassociate? Cut off that part of me so I would not feel it any more. I would leave my body so I did not have to see what was being done to it/me. In reclaiming me and allowing that little girl in me to be, I go into my body and feel what was being done to me a long time ago. As I am doing this I love and embrace me in that time back when it was happening. As I am embracing myself/that part of me, i.e.: my wrist that was being pulled so tight, I could not any longer feel my hand, I visualize and see who is grabbing me and I cry and claw that hand off of me. I peel and dig those fingers from my wrist and I tell that person not to touch me. I do this as if it is happening in this moment and then when I do get those fingers off of me, I rub my sore wrist and love my wrist until it feels much better. Multiple Sclerosis is made up of numb feelings in the extremities and I wake up and feel this numbness. This process is a very slow moving process. People want quick responses/quick fixes. They want instant relief from their pain. They do not want to feel any discomfort. I say it took a long time to create the dis/ease so it will take a similar amount of time to reverse the happening. I can't believe that I have been embarrassed and afraid to say to the world that I have found a way to heal from M.S. Who would believe me any way? Some maybe.

At the University they are spending so much money looking for an instant cure for M.S. They won't find one because it is not instant. There is much pain in re- healing thyself. Just think of how upset the pharmaceutical companies would be if I were able to get this information to the world. My healing technique does not include drugs of any kind. I've been pretending again, I've been afraid to tell the people these things because I have been afraid of them boohooing me. I did once try to say something to a Doctor at the M.S. conference; he wouldn't give me the time of day. Of course not. He is the one that has to find the answer to this incurable disease. Play words, in - curable in - cure - able dis - ease, go in to become cured. Neat eh? How many will get that?? Some maybe but I bet the western medical profession does not get it. At least not in this century. I hope when they do, someone shows them that I already had it. Yes, I want credit for what I have discovered.

Seems that my journal is full of teasers for my audience. (March 29, 2009. I'm reading this and having a wee chuckle.) I'm wondering where her perceived audience is this is how my mind works. Always running from place to place, from situation to situation. I need to find some space and time just for me to write.

I'd thought that today I would have some time just for me to write. I'd thought that today I would have some time but, my son has called from the school and he needs to come home with a headache.

I'm very aware of the growth and fears that are in me. For some reason I am giving a certain client a great deal of power. This client is an IV user, Supposedly past. I am not too sure about this though. I have felt abused by her and find it difficult to not be her victim. What does she represent from my past that creates this fear in me? What do I project her way? She is abusive and uneducated but I should be able to handle this situation. I need to be grounded and centered to meet with her the day after tomorrow.

When I was little they would tie me on the sacrifice table and put a needle in my arm so that my body would relax. So why am I getting lost in the past with this client? Obviously I have some unfinished business in this area. But if I lose it on Wednesday I could harm myself. This woman is abusive and she is feeling an injustice done to her. I will listen to her and how she feels but I will not set how I feel aside. Yet she will not hear because I have already expressed my thoughts to her. She only hears and sees her paranoia. She is very vulnerable and I feel vulnerable by her constant projections and dumping on me. How can I protect me from her? I need to be in my professional self and see her in her vulnerability. I need to not let her attacks put me off center. This is how she keeps people out of her space.

I'm remembering an exercise that we did in class around abusive people doing their therapy. Pushing the focus off of themselves by putting the focus elsewhere and when one is being attacked the focus goes to self for protection. So, see her style in how she maneuvers the focus, watch it and take note of it. Notice how vulnerable she must be to have to work so hard to change the focus, not to have it on her. I wonder what happened to her when she let herself have some attention. She has definitely pushed my buttons. I let her push them.

My going into a defensive mode makes me feel angry. I feel really angry that I have even had the need to be defensive at the program and me. I have let her dump her shit on me. I remember talking to Caroline and saying that I'd just as soon flush this woman down the toilet as have her in our program. Yet, if handled right this could be a break through for me as well as for her. I must have got in some how for her to be going to such lengths to push me away. Sort of like what is happening to me with my friend Jerry.

So there is a lesson for me to learn in this place. Yuck, always lessons. Can't a person ever take time off from learning? When I go into a defensive mode, all I want to do is put out my claws and attack. Fight back. So why do her actions help me to go into such a fighting, spitting place? Maybe because I have spent most of my life being a victim. Yes?... So, I am to see her vulnerability and appreciate it. Let her do what she needs to do and respect what she needs to say. No, I don't have to respect it, I can appreciate it. Just see her out there all by herself and afraid. It must take a great deal of courage to share the things that she is sharing.

Understand and share the rules of our program with her. Tell her if I feel attacked by her and let her know if I feel abused by her. Let her know that this is not acceptable behaviour and that I do not accept it. I cannot get lost in this process. There is so much fear for me. Old fear. Having fear of something that happened a very long time ago. I'd felt like a cornered kitten then and again I experience similar feelings.

This client's counsellor has just called me. Most interesting conversation. Seems that all of my fears are also her fears. So in this place she is a mirror of myself. I've decided that I would like Carol to also be at this meeting. This counsellor will be there. I need to get past my fear. I put out that I was feeling afraid of this client. That I was not feeling qualified to work with her. The counsellor shared many of the client's fears with me as well. Seems that the client is extremely ashamed. I was right though; if we can get past this situation we might have an opportunity to really do some work. Which ever way this turns out will be the way it needs to be. We are both cats that have been cornered and have our claws out. I wonder who will go first in the meeting? Who will come creeping out of the corner first? Maybe I should tell her that I sort of feel like I'm in a corner also. See past my fear. I definitely feel alive, right now. To much energy I've been giving to this situation. It is not over yet. Yuck. Yuck.

Lately I've been having many dreams. The bodywork is helping to open up much more for me. Having dreams of letting go of Jerry. We are in different worlds now. I do my agonizing out here in the world and she does hers as she is committed to the psych. world. Who's hiding from whom?

(2009 and a thought in regards to my asking who's hiding from whom? Perhaps no one is hiding but only doing it the way each person chooses to do it.)

I've felt powerful/strong, as I work with my new client here at my office. We are doing a trade. She gets hypnosis and reclaiming and I get bodywork. It's the perfect trade for me right now. I need to find my power/strength right now. I need to get into a place inside of me where I feel strong. Yet I have a feeling that when we do begin on Wednesday, there will again be this fear for me. Maybe it will be her fear. Isn't it interesting that all the while that I was going through that earlier, that the counsellor then calls me? Goddess, can I be so open that I receive all of that information? For it to be so powerful for me there has to be unfinished business. I want to put more energy into this journal. I want to get it moving so I can share it with the world. Now that I've decided that I don't have to hide the fact that I have found a way to heal me of Multiple Sclerosis. I feel excited. I bet there are others like me who have done similar things. Will I be the one that comes out though?

(March 28, 2009: my opinion about personal power is, it is not real. Power is an ego creation and we can move beyond this.)

Feb. 25, 1990

5 years ago my mother died. She had a heart attack and was alone when she died. There was no family, or someone to love her,

with her when she died. This makes me feel sad inside of me. How can life end like this? To be all alone and die.

I've been ill these past few days. Since that fear that came up for me. The client did not show up for the meeting. We all were there and she did not arrive. Seems that she has disappeared. Now I have a 3-bedroom town house that is full of her furniture and I need to do something about it. I'm glad that I was able to get past the fear in me and go to this meeting. Sad that she could not.

I'm feeling quite dizzy these past 2 days and I went to see my doctor last Friday and was put on antibiotics. Maybe they are what are making me dizzy. I booked off the last 2 days and have stayed home in bed.

I miss my mom. So many things that I have done and she's not been here to share with. The last few years I remember how she would listen to me. I would always call her and tell her things about the kids and what ever else that was going on of importance. My throat is sore and I feel choked up right now. Momma, we did have a special relationship. I was so very afraid of you. But there was another side to us. My fear was of the past when you were crazy and did all of those horrible things to me. I guess because they were locked up in my unconscious mind I was always a little frightened of you. How could I love a mother so very much who did those things to me? You were my momma and I loved you.

If only you could help me. I now have so much difficulty getting near my older son. It's as if I can't even touch him, just like you couldn't touch me. I want to make this different. I do not want him to have to do without his mother's touch all of his life like I did. How can I get close to him now when he is almost 17 years old? He doesn't know how to touch or to cry. How can I help him? He is my child. I love him.

Life is a vicious circle. It goes around and around, never ending and hardly ever changing. I am tired. So very tired of this circle. It is time for me to say good night for this night. I am spacey and dizzy right now. So I say good night 'Reace. You are.

March 1, 1990

My Eyes

I am a traveler, a visitor.
I have the ability to focus like a lens and make things happen, change and alter.
I can open doors with a push. I can close them too.
Thought is the essence of where I am now.
Thought is the essence of movement.
I hold a key ... to an answer.
I must find the door.
My mission is to find the door ... to alter the knowledge.
My thought, with my lens focus, is the movement.
I move.
I am the thought. Whose thought?
Thought opens doors and closes them too.
When will I know?
When will I???

One day I wrote these thoughts. I don't remember when. I thought that I would include them. When I say push, I don't mean that I actually physically push a door. I am sharing from a place of energy. Not all persons know this place that things happen, alter. It is a special place that I know of. My thoughts are energy.

This feels as if it is a time out. I had not planned on being here today. I am glad that I have come to this place inside of me. I feel rested here and not troubled. My night time dreams are full of nurturing. In my dreams there are men who comfort me and care for me.

When I wrote the poem I had thought of the word door and what it meant. Those words and thoughts are what came from me. Now I see a window. I suppose I should look out the window. That is what windows are for, yes? When I am ready a window opens inside of me, so that I can see. I see riches and light and I feel warm. I live in a mansion in me. I decide what I should be before I come out to play.

The door is open and the breeze is blowing in. Spring is coming. I see further and I see more of what there is to see. I feel confined inside. Always looking out. Staying inside of myself and looking out. I need to leave this mansion and go out and play for a while. I will come back to be inside of me but I need to go out for awhile and play and float in the sunshine and feel the wind on my face. To fly is what I need to do. It has been so long.

The door is open. I can go out and I can come in. Even though I've been so very busy out in the world. I've still been in a prison inside of me. A long time ago the door opened and I left a room that I had hidden in. Now the door to the mansion is open and I can go outside of the house in me. It has taken me so very long to arrive at this place in me.

All of the work that I've done and still have yet to do. What a story this is becoming eh? Wild yes? These are the thoughts that interrupt what I do. The ones that play the judge for me. I suppose I still need to keep me in line. With what thought? I'm free. I'm free. I need to stop for now.

March 2

The sun is shining outside and it is warm. I talked with the woman I've begun an exchange with. I told her I feel as if I've let go of something that I no longer need and that I feel like I would like to go deeper into me. I will see her tomorrow for me. The deeper that I go, the more still I be. Come. The more content I get. Part of me is here typing and a part of me is outside in the sun listening to the birds. I need to go out there now.

I'm floating right now and this feels nice. My friend Ron is coming to visit with me for awhile. A most curious experience for me to have a male friend who I can talk to and feel safe with. Very curious for me this is. Between last eve and this day I have read all that I have written in this journal. I seem to be doing a dance with myself. I'm at the beginning of me. I'm going to go deeper into me soon. What will I find? Who?? Maybe this is more like it. I notice that people have begun to have names in my story the last while. I'm becoming less and less afraid to have people in my life.

I received a letter yesterday requesting additional information on our project. This is promising, yes?

I hope that the sun shines all weekend because on Sunday I would like to go down to the beach for a nice walk. This would be good. I feel as if I am not really here. In and out at the same time. So many things to share and I can't find much of anything right now.

March 3

More and more, I am here in the present. It seems that it is safer for me to be in the present than back in the past. I was in the city today. I went to have my bracelet designed and then off to have bodywork. I'm having a gold cuff with crescent moons and stars put on the face. I feel the need to cry tonight. I do not know what this is all about. My house is quiet. So very quiet. So why can I not experience this quiet? Why do I always need to be so busy?

A little later.

There is this empty hole inside of me. A space that has an ache in it. I have spent some time with me and a special magic friend. My face is tear stained. I guess I just need to feel this space for a time. Then I will find some wonderful newness to fill it with. This magic friend that I have is the one that I had begun my journey with at the start. He is special to me, for me. I think that I have already mentioned him in my journal.

My right ear is plugged right now. There is a ringing in it. I feel as if I have been slapped real hard across the right side of my head. So that I can hardly hear out of my ear.

How do little children ever make it to grow into adults? Good question. Most of the little children get large bodies, but inside they are still children. Ask a few so called grown ups and they will tell you. They do not feel old at all. Sometimes I feel as if I were a very small child and then other times I feel as if I am 100 years of age.

I was just thinking of when we lived up North when I was 5 through 8 years old and I end up feeling sick to my stomach. There were some awful ugly things that happened when we lived up there. I remember being strapped into a high chair. I got to sit outside in the sun while I was strapped into a high chair. I had big sores on my thighs between my legs. They left scars on me. I was always getting some sort of infection. I'm not at all surprised with what I was subjected to. More than likely I had a venereal disease of some sort. My folks were weird, strange people.

Mar. 4

Hard to find a quiet place in me. So many distractions. People, lots of people talking, walking and making noise. I'm at the beach. The sun is warm and bright. The breeze is nice and soft. Birds, lots of birds all around. The sand is cool under me and the water, well the water is quiet. How can I shut the noises of people out? The birds are talking and squawking. Everything smells so nice. The boats look peaceful. The dogs and cats out to play. Children running through the water. White puffy clouds in the blue ski. Time for me to walk.

Mar. 5

There is this uneasiness in me. A feeling of, where is 'Reace in all of the confusion? I have difficulty figuring out how I can be so competent as a professional and have this scattered feeling inside of me. Just good at setting myself aside, eh? So what else is new?

This need to scream is in me. The injustices that have been done. I need to throw a tantrum, yes I need to throw a good old fashioned tantrum. Where is all of this anger coming from? Feeling crowded. Masking, not expressing me. Maybe if I allowed myself to go into the anger, I just might find out what it is all about. I will let me scream when I'm out in my car tonight. On my way to the meeting I will scream.

My body is full of this rage. Not so much frustration as it is the rage. RAGE, RAGE, RAGE, RAGE, RAGE, RAGE. I could write a page of rage. I feel like tearing up something. Get a baseball bat and pound the ground with it. Could use Bob's padded room right now. I wonder if he would lend it out for a few minutes unsupervised. Just so I could throw my tantrum. He probably would if I asked him.

There was a great deal of movement in my shoulder area when I was getting the shiatsu treatment. Yuck. I hate admitting that I have all of this anger in me. I feel embarrassed about expressing the anger. My anger. I've watched as others have expressed anger and it looks dumb. My perception. It looks ugly also. But most important, it is frightening and it terrifies me.

So if nobody sees me be angry then I can pretend that I do not have this emotion. What a conflict there is in me over anger. Would be a major breakthrough if I could consciously have my anger validated, wouldn't it? Yuck. Will I ever get there. Maybe I could tell someone, I don't have to show them.

What a joke. If I hadn't been angry all of this time, I would never had made it as far as I have. I get so mad and so bored that I make something. Like a kid would make a sandcastle, I make a non-profit society. Then I get bored because it gets hard. I have a headache.

Mar. 6

Hi! It's me again. Are you surprised. I've started to tell some people that my parents were Satan worshipers and that I was a sacrifice for them to use. I'm feeling a little uncomfortable telling the secrets of my past that I have hidden so carefully. Even from me I have hidden them.

Lately I've been feeling the need to return up North where we hid for 3 years, from what? What happened in 1955 that we had to go up to the mountain to live. My dad worked in the mill while we lived up there. But why did my mom lose her hair? When someone loses their hair it is usually from too much stress. I need to remember that I had a past. I need to know that I had a childhood.

I question why I find the need to share that I had such a crazy, weird past. Am I cracking up? Am I? Why is it so hard to tell? There is no one to punish me now. To own all of one's self is probably the most difficult quest of all.

So maybe I need to tell people that I am not a freak. I did not do those things. They were done to me. I need to be real. To not pretend that I come from the perfect background. It is my belief that there is not a person on this planet that comes from the perfect background. I'm feeling very real right now. I can see that the people pretend. They all do in one way or another. I am in sane. I like this. I am in side and I have become in sane. You have to go in to be come sane. Yes???

I know this place well. When I was little I would come to this place in me and pretend that the world outside wasn't there. My magic place in me where all things were wonderful and perfect. I'm starting to remember some more. I know because I am and have been on my way into a memory for a little while now. Only thing is, I have just become aware of this.

I have reread the last bit that I wrote and it tells me, maybe the pieces that have been on the news are helping me to remember. Who knows, maybe it has to do with the time of the year. I see a little girl on a table in the middle of a room. She lays so very still and she does not make one peep.

She is such a good little girl. She just lays there in her own world while the other world does not touch her. What a strong little girl she is. They do not kill her because she is not really there. Her mind has gone somewhere else but I can see her laying on that table. She has a doll to play with. A very special doll. One that has magic in her. The magic to focus out the rest of the world. No wonder I can focus my eyes like a camera lens and see only what I focus on. I've been told that some people go to the east to train to learn how to meditate and focus the way that I do. I learned how to do this to survive when I was little. You have to block so well that there is nothing out there at all.

I can see you on that table little girl. You are somewhere else aren't you little girl? I am standing beside you and you can't see me. You are not crazy little one, you have just gone somewhere far inside of you. What have you seen little one? Can you remember? I would like you to remember and come out and tell me what you have seen. Maybe if I just pick you up and hold you with me. Your mind has snapped in this place, hasn't it little girl? I'm here now. I wasn't here when you went through this because I was not here.

"I remember when I was very small that I had a magic mom. She was like you. A lady was there. I know you. You were there when I was little. I used to talk to you when I went inside. They used to wonder who I was talking to. You were the magic lady who kept me alive. I knew that you were real. As I grew I always knew that someone had stepped in to help me. It was you. I thought you were a lady outside of me. I did not know that you lived in me. I did have someone to help me. YOU! Who are YOU? I can't see what they are doing out there".

I'm not going to look tonight because my son is calling me and I am feeling as if I have already journeyed in me quite far. I need a day where I can go in and not upset anyone else. I need to be just with me. So, I am going to end for this night and I will come back to this place soon. I'm going out now to give my son his massage. See you.

Mar. 11

My chest is swollen with grief (Phlegm). This day has been a very difficult day. For some reason I've needed to take on more than I should. Some others have issues with me. Or at least they think that it is me. For some reason for awhile I needed to take these things on. As if I need any more. My way of drowning myself in self pity. My throat is sore again. Yesterday I again had some work done on my body and this is what is moving things in me. I know that this is so.

It has been quite some time since I have allowed me to cry and feel and express my pain. I know that this is what I need to do. The moon is full tonight and she is beautiful, I was outside and said to the moon that I want to go, I do not want to be here any longer. I say these words and the tears well up in my eyes. I am so very tired of being on this planet and playing and pretending this game called life. I watch the news on TV and it is so very crazy. How can so many children be starving to death? This is life? This is an experience that is necessary for us on this planet to learn? I do not understand.

My throat aches to scream. I want to pack my bags and move on. I feel stuck in this place, in this world. On this plane. I want a new script. What one now? What will I do? This world is not large enough. I want more to play with. I'm tired of working so hard and getting nothing for my work. I'm always poor and I should not be for all of this work that I give to the world. My car is falling apart and I can't even purchase a new one on the income that I receive. Why can I not have an income? Why do I only let me just get by? All I ever seem to do is bitch and complain.

I used to take pleasure from so many of the things that I do. Now I feel used and dumped on. I am disappointed with life. In a nut shell this is what I feel, disappointed with human kind and with me. I'm not even getting school credits for what I am doing now. I get nothing. My patience is about worn completely thin. Maybe I should talk to someone about how I am feeling. Not many want to listen to so much anger. Outrage and more. It is hard to set me aside when I am feeling so strong in an emotion.

Is all of this anger coming from the emotion that I have begun to feel from the place of seeing the little girl on that table? I wonder. Can I let her have this emotion? Can I teach her how to say stop?

Mar. 21

Where do the days go? I do wonder. Last week I was called to go in to a transition house. A woman who was escaping from a satanic cult had arrived. I met this woman and spent over an hour with her. I was able to join her with the memories of my past. If nothing else I have shown her that it is possible to get away from these people. She said to me, "but you're so pretty and you look normal". I said I am normal. To put into words what happened for me while I was with this woman is difficult. I have a feeling of a great breakthrough in myself. I am different again. I feel as if I have come through a world and into new one. I had a sense of going through a veil of energy. I turned around and looked at what I had come through and saw a world that I was no longer a part of. This was an exciting feeling for me. I felt as if I had read a book and it was finished. That story is complete for me and I am no longer a part of it. I am no longer living that life.

What an odd sense this has given me inside of myself. It is as if I never even lived that life. I did though. Because I was able to be with that woman at the transition house. I knew that it was now her story. She wanted to know how I was able to get away from them. I said that I just left and they can't touch me any more. I said to her that I remember when they cut the kitties head off and drained the blood. I looked at her and her eyes were vacant. I asked her where she went. She said, "Somewhere safe." I said, "yes I know the place you went to".

While I was with her I talked to maybe 5 different people in her body. I knew because I have been there. The only way to survive is to become more than one inside of yourself. She is one of what they call the baby factories. They breed her and use the infant as a sacrifice. She is pregnant again. No wonder she runs. The blood of the infant, they believe is powerful. They are confused, the life of the infant is powerful. Since I have been with this woman I have been disclosing that I was subjected to a satanic childhood. This part is OK for me to do now. It was "past tense", am no longer a part. Through this woman I have embraced another part of myself. Thank you to her for this part of me. I sat with this for two days before I was able to get clear, it was so powerful for me to experience this day.

May 2, 1990

My grandma is dead. She died on April 18. My friend Ronny gave me some of his bonus points and he booked me a flight so that I could go be with gram before she died. I flew in on the Friday and out again on Saturday. I sat with gram and rubbed her feet so that she would be comfortable. She told me she wouldn't let them take her gangrened leg off as she was going to walk into heaven on two feet. I watched her come in and out of this world.

My Aunt welcomed me into her home and took me back and forth to the hospital to see gram. One day I will be able to give back to her some of what she gave to me. My mother's sister. I felt as if I was not an orphan when I was with her. I hurt inside so much.

I got a card from my friend Jerry today. Maybe this is why it is finally alright to be in touch with how I'm feeling about grandma dying.

It has been so long since I have been inside so deep. She is the only one that I have let into this deep place outside of the occasional therapist. I miss her very much. My grandma turned 91 years on the Monday and then she died on Wednesday. I would write her letters and ask her to be the one to be proud of me and now she is gone. I feel so alone. All of the power that I have. Power. What is power anyway? My new position. On the Minister of Women's Programs Advisory Council. She is only a woman. No more than you or I. She hurts just as I do. The abuse that other women give out is horrible. I watch as a group abused the Minister and I. They say that they are fighting to prevent abuse of woman and then they use extreme abuse. They do not or are not aware that they are even doing this to each other. So what can I do to help stop this?

Tomorrow I again board the helijet for the next advisory committee meeting. This is an exciting perk for me. Yet the abuse that I am being subjected to is intolerable. How long has it been since I have been in this place for me? I must find some time to get into me again. Seems that I've been giving me away again.

May 21, 1990

So, Hello again to me. My story does no longer flow. But neither does my life lately. I've been ill now for a few days. Doing too much work and not getting myself nourished enough to balance the work. Today only my head hurts. It feels as if a vice is holding onto my head and squeezing it hard.

I mowed the front lawn today and this was good for me. I need much more of the every day earth stuff in my life. I feel more alive and human if I do earth work. I need to take a long holiday away from the head work. Some of my clients are awfully abusive in their projecting their unfinished internal work. It makes it so hard to move forward with so much muck in the way. I'm tired.. I think that I will let them take care of what is bothering them. The trouble is, they are being so very destructive and criticizing towards all that we try and do. So lets stop trying to do anything at all. I am going to let them work out things for themselves. When I was a client, I do not recall being so abusive to the people that were trying to help me.

Trying to do too many things all at one time is my biggest fault. I have been losing center of myself.

I had another call from my father of origin's girlfriend. The first time that she called, she called pretending to be a woman needing assistance from an abusive relationship. (maybe she is in an abusive relationship) I referred her on to first stage transition for the help that she was asking for. She called again, this time sharing that she lived with my father. There were many concerns that she was asking after. Mostly she found it strange that a daughter would simply walk out of her father's life never to return. She wanted to know, so I told her that in fact I did have an incestuous background. She said that she could never be with a man who had been with a little girl. I wished her luck and told her that only she knew what was best for her.

She called again last week. This time with a request. She wanted to know if I knew someone that he (father) could go and see to get some help for his problem. I said that I would do some homework on this and call her back as soon as I knew.

I did do some homework. I phoned the transition house where a woman worker in fact used to work in the prison system. I asked her if she knew anyone who worked with pedophiles. She gave me a number to call. I called the number. I left my name and phone number.

The next day, a man called me. He was from the institution. I know that he works with people like my father. He (father) did request a referral after all. I got a little fuzzy while I was on the phone with the man. I told him that I am a Community Social Service Worker and the Developer of a second-stage transition house for battered women and their children and that presently I am on the Provincial Minister's Advisory Council for women. I suppose I needed to hang on to something. I felt as if I were getting lost. I had not intended for it to be anything other than me looking for information on who was available.

Two days later, it dawns on me that I in fact reported my father. The ministry of Social Services will be contacted now. The man (Russ) will call me back on Tuesday. He had said, I don't like to leave you like this. He had been aware of my being disconcerted. I heard him. He was concerned about me. I had also said that I was 40 years old now and this had happened along time ago. I had also said that my father was in his 70's now. I won't really be 40 until next August. Russ has concerns that after all of these years why would he want help now? Has he in fact done something and has become frightened? Goddess, I hope he has not hurt another little girl. But I know that he has, there have been many little girls along the way that he has hurt. Sick, Sick man.

I've been noticing all of the movies that have been on these past few days. A lot of them are about little girls and boys being hurt sexually. Oh goddess, I just want to bury myself and make it all go away. Bury myself... Isn't that what I in fact did for 33 years? I'm losing hope. Really losing hope. This whole world is full of abuse. My whole world is full of abuse. I am hanging on to the end of a rope. Seems that the only time that I have time to write in my journal is when I am in this place. Like a last place of hope for me. Me. Being me.

A client had said that she had been promised an abuse free environment. There is no abuse free environment on this planet. The difference for me is that I am open and I feel and I hear the things that do go on in this world. I am getting lost in it all though. There is too much. So this means that I need to find another avenue for nourishment. I am tired of working. Yes, I do need a holiday.

So, will I ever finish this story? Somehow I do not think so. Maybe when I die it will be over. I'm thinking of letting someone read what I have written.

May 27, 1990

I'm having a quiet day today. Feeling a little frustrated with not having something to do. So as I can focus outside of me.

I've told my story to a social worker and she in turn called head office to pass on the information. I also shared that I am writing a book. The social worker asked what the title would be and when the book would in fact be out to the public? She wants to get a copy. She said it will help many people. The second worker that called asked, WHY? after all of these years do you want to report this? I in turn said that I had not consciously planned this but my father's girlfriend had asked if I could find some help for his problem. Looks like I've really come out now. There is no turning back at all.

My friend Ronny suggested that I must make another copy of these writings. Just in case something happened to what I've already written. There is no way I could repeat what I've said so far. I will do so, as he suggested.

A little girl who was not allowed to be. I've sure showed them that they can't stop me from being. For some reason I have a need to curl up in someone's arms and cry. I had a wonderful day yesterday when I went out with Ron. Maybe being held a little while has made me get in touch with how much I would like to have arms to hold me available all of the time whenever I need them. Yes, that is probably it.

Not long now and I will graduate from the Community Social Service Worker Program. I am looking forward to this. Some say to me, 'Reace, what will you do after you graduate? If you are doing all that you are now, what can you do after? Interesting question. I guess I have felt as if I have been rehearsing for what is to come. Whatever that will be. Who knows? Tomorrow evening I step down from the president's chair of the transition housing program. Time to move on to other things.

Yesterday, before I met with Ron, I had gone to see Anna to have a Jin Shin Do treatment. For some time I have been working with Anna now and it is getting safer for my body to relax and begin to remember. This time as I began to remember it is different than before. Before if I remembered something it was like watching a bad movie. Now as I lay on the table in her office, I have this feeling as though things are coming to me like they are a part of me. It is like putting the negative and the picture together. Like I am going into the picture of what was and not just watching it. Instead of just touching it for a few moments as I view what I see, I am it. I am beginning to not disassociate from what I so long ago lived. I lay on the table in Anna's office while she worked and I felt as if the worlds were beginning to come together. She would encourage me to stay present while she worked, to feel what the feelings were and view the images that I saw.

I remember being on the table when I was little. There was a rope around my ankle, my right ankle. I can feel it now. I also sensed a sucking animal that looked like a blob of some sort, on my ankle. Like a huge leach or something. I was drugged and there was an IV in my arm to keep me drugged. All I could do was watch. It was different though. I am her. It is not just a picture that I see. Awe, I get it. I am beginning to integrate that little girl and claim all that she experienced as all I experienced in my childhood.

Finally telling on daddy and he can't hurt me no more. But can he? He still denies that he ever did anything to me. I am afraid some. Yes I am. All sorts of tapes in my head. If you tell now and he did do some things I could be responsible because I knew for a long time what kind of men (yes, men as he was multiple) he was. Seems I heard those words before. Oh well, someone had to tell, tell, tell. And I had to make it safe enough for the little girl in me to do these things. For me to do these things. I know it is not going to be easy for me in the next while. There will be lots of angry people because I told.

I'm making people do extra work too. That's OK. This is what their job is. They have enough work to do though. All of these old tapes. Yes, many of them are true but this is their job and I finally am strong enough to tell. I have credibility now. Yes, I have credibility now. People will listen to me now. They wouldn't listen then. After all, my mother was a registered nurse and my father a member of the church. They had respectability. I did not even have a voice then.

I think it is great that the school of nursing is doing research on the children's experience of living in an abusive environment. They are going to let the children talk without their parents listening. I'm glad for the children but I hope the professionals don't tell on the children so that they end up being beaten and locked in a closet.

I phoned my brother after I had talked with the Social Worker. I had let him know that I had done this. His reaction was one of support for what I had done but also the fear came. He wanted to know if the ministry was going to take precautions to protect us from what is to come. I said, Donald, he can't hurt us now. He is old and weak. Interesting that the fear had not left for both of us. We are both adults now and yet because the horrors were so powerful they still come into our adult life. I wonder how my little brother, Curt, will react when he finds out that the ministry has talked with his little girl. Will he be frightened? Will he be angry? Will he wake up?

I find it hard to write. I feel tired after I've written just two pages. My little girl is getting angry. I can see her in me. She wants to tear that animal off her ankle and throw it away. To rip the needle out of her arm and tear it up. To tell those horrible people that they are all a bunch of fruit cakes. Talk about weird people. Hanging a little girl upside down by one ankle. So that the stuff that they stuffed her with wouldn't fall out.

When I was 27 they took my uterus out and packed me with a sulpha packing. I had a violent reaction to being packed. My body was probably remembering. Get that awful junk out of me. I don't want it in me. Get it out..... To stop the bleeding I was packed both times. Hung upside down. To stop the bleeding. Wasn't that nice of them? At least I didn't bleed to death.

May 29, 1990

Last evening was my final board meeting as president for the local transition house. Our annual general meeting and I stepped down. We all went out for a drink after and visited for awhile. I've been asked to stay connected to some and I think that I will. I do believe that I had inside begun to remove myself awhile ago. I do not feel any different today than yesterday. Knowing me, there is some powerful significance in what I did do in stepping down. I will miss chairing those meetings though. I hope they miss me for awhile anyway.

June 2, 1990

Dreams and day memories. I have been experiencing some numbness in the top part of my right foot and lower part of me leg. The numbness is patchy. I see and feel me being dragged and carried to the table for the Satan service. Other memories also haunting me. Me being taken to a gravel pit and when the wonderful father arrived to clean the dirt and blood off of me.

They had my legs pulled apart and they were holding onto my ankles. They were holding onto my wrists also. I would try and wiggle away. I was not cooperating very well. I was placed on the table and held there. My legs were pulled apart and my ankles were tied. My hands were put into cuffs or something. I remember screaming. This is strange because I did not have a voice then. The one that was there did. A needle went into my arm and my thigh and soon I did not feel. But I could see. When I was a teenager, I would always wear a lot of eye makeup to show off my eyes. This would really bug my dad. I wanted him to see that I had eyes.

I had eyes but I had no memory. My unconscious was at work. A part of me knew. How did I survive? By going away. It does not make sense. What did they expect to accomplish? There is no sense. Playing doctor. There were lights and rubber gloves. No, I woke up on a table in a doctor's office. Will I ever be clear in this place inside of me? So many parts of my life are missing.

The gravel pit I used to drive by as an adult and always there was this uncomfortable feeling when I saw a gravel pit. Then I began to hallucinate and see a little girl standing, crying and covered in dirt and blood. He would take me there and hurt me. I was cold and frightened. The rocks hurt my little bum. Then I was alone and hurt. I stood up and looked up at the heavens and silently was angry with the gods. How could they be so mean to me? How could they leave a little girl all alone in the night? Then he would come and rescue me. Oh wasn't he the most wonderful daddy to find me and save me? He would always have something there to clean me with. He would wrap me in a blanket to warm me. I would be numb from shock and cold. I keep seeing more to the picture all of the time now. (I just got (Nov. 15/92) that my father set it up so that I could not trust the gods. He gave me those thoughts about the gods.) One day I will have all of the pieces to my puzzle.

June 3

Today's paper has almost a full page article about me and what I am doing. Disclosing parts of my past and who I am Eek. I read the article and proceed to break out in a sweat.

I'm off this afternoon for another meeting of the Advisory Council on Community Based Programs for Women. This is to be our last meeting on this project. A very growing experience this has been for me. There is still this little person inside of me that is amazed at what is happening in my life. How? When? Did I get to this place?..

A strange dream last eve. I was at my hotel and my ex spouse arrived as a part of the team. For some reason we ended up sharing a room. There were two queen sized beds. In the night he pushed the beds beside each other. He rolled over in his sleep and landed on top of me. I woke because I was being smothered and I could not breath. Somehow I wiggled from under his weight and squiggled out the left side of the bed. He woke as I was leaving. Said that he needed to be close in order to sleep. He was getting aroused and I said settle down. I woke up soon after this.

A long time ago, well not that long ago really, when I was doing some therapy around my ex, I realized that for me, he represented my anger. A part of me that I would not nor could not own. Me and my anger coming together somehow. But it is smothering me and I need to find a way NOT to STOP BREATHING when I experience ANGER. I must give my anger life inside of my body. Air is free. The weight was great also. Right now my chest is hurting. Grief in me. Just last week I approached my ex's partner in regards to he and I maybe getting together for coffee. One day we will be grandparents to the same children and things would be a great deal easier if we could communicate a bit easier. He has not gotten back to me in regards to this request. First I accept this part of me in my dream and then I embrace it in my waking world.

June 9, 1990

I did some work today. I was with Anna and while she was giving me shiatsu, I began releasing a memory. I began with quiet tears beginning to flow down my cheeks. Then seeing began. I saw a dead animal. I do not know what kind yet. All that was standing out was that it had been sliced open and it smelled awful. Someone was holding me and pushing me forward. They had my foot and wanted to put it in the animal.

"I don't want it in there. I don't I don't. Stop doing that to me."

They did put my foot in it. I remember in my head stopping that from being my foot. Trying desperately to not feel what was happening to me. Today, I did not let go of my foot. I saw all of that blood and felt it on my foot and leg. I wiped it off. I cried for the little girl in me who had to go through that. I do not understand why??? No sense, no sense, does not make any sense. My foot and lower leg are still numb. Not all of the feeling has returned. I hugged me because the little girl inside of me hurts so much. It will take some time to heal this part of me. I will give me the time that I need. I know now that, I am alone. This is Okay.

June 16/90

Another week has gone by. Again I was in to see Anna and have her work on me with Shiatsu. I felt new when I got there. When I had started to go in to the old place last week, I had said that I was frightened because before when this happened I would get amnesia. I would just be there with no memories of any life at all. I felt as if this shift was again happening inside of me and I did not want to lose all that I have learned in the past 6.5 years. The newness came and I did not lose the knowing that I had inside of me. This is different for me.

This new part of me that came back was the part of me that did have amnesia. On one level inside of me I do feel as if I have amnesia and yet I remember who I've been for the last while. This is curious, very curious. I feel disconcerted in me. One difference that I am becoming aware of is that when I go out into the world I do not set myself aside for others. (March 6, 2009. Wow, I can't believe I said this as I've become aware of I do set me aside for another person on a regular basis. Bob says, "First comes the awareness") I stay present in me and be there for the other Yes, this is more like the truth. This is different. Usually I would become the place that I am at or the person that I am with. People got used to this. Now I/me is there also. This is called meeting yourself, yes? Growing up inside of yourself is a long journey.

I do not understand all that has taken place inside of me and so I will give myself time to adjust to the newness. I do find it interesting that a part of me knew and said out loud, all of what I was used to happening, when I went into that old place inside of me.

Tomorrow is father's day and I have no feeling in me about it, I was writing last year and was remembering things that had to happen on daddy's special day, I wonder if he has been caught yet? If my reporting him has made a difference in his life. It has made a difference in my life. My fear of him has lifted. Now all I have left in me are all of the memories of before. I've decided that if this goes to court around my little niece, I will testify against my father of Origin. Then the little girl in me can have her day in a court of law where she will be safe inside of me. I will do it for my niece and for me.

Later

I watched a movie tonight. This woman in the movie was in an accident and lost all of her memory before the accident because of brain damage. She had to start her life all over again without ever remembering her past. Maybe I should just let it all go. It is hard to try and remember and fill in all of the blanks of my past. If I remember I remember, if not I'll just take each day as it comes. I guess that is how I have been living. It is like I had this really bad dream. It is over, that dream and a new one has begun.

The amnesia is strong for me right now. Maybe because things are coming in. This emptiness is great inside of me. I play the play out there, but it is just a play. For awhile I get lost in the play and play it as if my life depended on it. I suppose it does. And, now I have come out of the play. Wondering, wondering who, what, where am I, do I and, am I? Only anger is in me now. When my anger is clear and focused I feel strong inside of me.

I am aware of the fact that I have yet to claim my body. Tonight I became aware of this. Noticing that I am not pleased with my body. Remembering when I was really thin and I still was not really pleased. Thinking that my body is only a toilet for all of the wastes that I put into it and all of the waste that I hold in it. It is only a vehicle.

But there is another faint voice that I hear in me. My body is me, but I do not know this on a conscious level. My head knows this but I do not know this. How could I be my body? My body is a house that I live in, that I carry my luggage in. I am not my body, my body is the house that I live in. Lots of attics inside that have trunks full of old antiques like in an old mansion. I go into the rooms and try on the old outfits and play dress up. But I am bored with the old outfits. I want new rooms and new outfits. Most of all I would like to be with my body instead of only residing in it, like I'm in a hotel or something. I would like my body to have less suitcases on it and in it. Like I've put all of this protection on me to keep the insides safe from harm.

I would like to look in a mirror and like who I see. To say hello to who I see and let her be OK. To really see me and learn to like me. Disassociation in the max. I look after my body fairly well, but I could look after it better.

June 22

Hello. A gypsy part of me seems to be here. I again have the need to wear black. It is hot outside. Summer has arrived again. Around and around we go. I hurt. So very much I hurt. So many self doubts inside of me. It seems I've retreated into myself. I feel as if I'm on the verge of a major breakthrough or something. To hold onto some sort of sanity is ever so hard. I put on a mask and out I go to meet others needs, when in me I have such great sorrow. My neck is stiff. I've been hanging on so tight.

We have to make things right inside of us and that we are OK and that we count. I am running out of patience for all of the people that continually bitch and complain instead of chipping in and helping out. This world spends so much of its time fighting, complaining, pulling those people down who begin to achieve something, not listening, attaching, destroying, hurting, and more. Where's the team effort? This world seems to think that it has come so very far. I say huh! Patience definitely seems to be what I need to learn in this lifetime.

I've been walking every day that I am not swimming. I'm beginning to feel better for this.

I've qualified for the RRAP program - a residential rehabilitation assistance program that help people upgrade their house so that it meets safety standards. I still do not make any money. This is why I qualify. I'm getting new carpets in my living room and hallway, my bathroom is getting redone, a new roof and a new kitchen counter. There is $600 left over that I want to spend having things painted. This will be so wonderful to have done.

I need to see Pharaoh and get a hug while I cry. My chest is burning.

June 25

On the morning of the 23rd, just before I went in to see Anna, I phoned Pharaoh. I just reread what I'd written the day before that. Seems I'd wanted to see Pharaoh and get a hug while I cried. Well, I phoned him and he did say that he would call and we would go out for lunch on a Friday. I hope he does call me. I need some magic in my life. He seemed quite pleased that I had not given up. He was laughing softly out loud. I asked him to look at the article that was in the newspaper about me. I hope that he liked it.

Drinking blood, drinking blood. I began to like the taste of it. Pieces of flesh on the tray and drinks of blood. I was such a good girl. I would hold the tray so well, I wouldn't spill as I passed the tray around to all of the big people.

"**Aren't I good.**" I would say. I was going to make a wonderful high priestess wasn't I? I knew how to cut the body so we could get the blood. I found a way to cut and not kill. I thought they would be pleased. It did not matter.

The school phoned. They want my younger son to go to summer school. He says no because he will not pass the math that he has already done for two years. I can see his point and so he will see his counsellor tomorrow and they will decide. I did tell him that I would give him the funds if he chooses summer school. I will support the decision that he makes. He is growing up and making some of his own choices now.

Another day has gone and I am quiet inside. I feel as if I am searching inside of myself for something. I do not know what yet. The changes are many for me. Feels like I'm leaving behind a period of my growth and moving into another area. Always growing and always changing. Calling Martin was a big step for me. Acknowledging that I have in fact moved into the professional world and am letting go of another stage. Gads, I keep shedding my skin. No wonder I feel so new. I hope that I wasn't calling Martin just to grab on to someone. That would not be fair to him. I do not think that I was doing that. I really would like to have a relationship with him.

Both of my children are weaning themselves from me as a mother. It is up to me to help them discover another way of relating with me. I need to treat them like men instead of my baby boys. Let them go and they will learn to fly on their own. Birds do, so they can too. I'll be 40 this summer. Do ages or stages help to make the changes happen in life? I think a little of both.

July 1, 1990

Lots of dreams and I have some recall of them. Not a great deal, but some. A huge fish coming after me. I throw fish in its way and he devours them. Just tears great chunks from them. I find this bench and I lift the seat and crawl inside. I lay with my back to the wall and I can see out. I close the lid. I'm safe in this place so I decide to go to sleep. A man is there and I tell him that there is this herb that will awaken me. I can't remember what the herb was. All of the evil and violence is outside and I am safe inside of the bench. It kind of reminds me of the world that we live in. Maybe I will understand this dream soon.

Today I went swimming. This day I swam 50 lengths of the pool. When I had begun the trip down to the pool I had flashbacks of me as a little girl at the pool. I was playing and having fun with other children. I saw my father come. My body went rigid. He needed me for something so he said. I did not want to leave the other children. We had been having fun. He pulled me out of the pool and pulled me with him. He took me into the gully, it was not far from the pool. I keep seeing more all of the time. These pictures come into my head. Like a bad dream, I want to look at the pictures and then I don't. I remember going back to the pool. I become invisible a few feet to the pool. Really into myself. Thinking that all of the children can see how dirty I am. I was acting strange towards them. So they would leave me alone. All alone again.

Lots of times he took me into the gully. I think once I saw a little girl all hurt and dead in the gully. I don't know if it was the little girl that really was killed in that town that I spent so many years. I know that I was not the only little girl that my father hurt. Sometimes I think that I am crazy and losing my mind. I did not want to go into that gully with my father. It is weird. I would leave the house that we lived in, I must have, and I would go through the gully to school. Strange because I don't ever remember being inside that house or going into that gully to get to school. I wonder if it is still there. I barely remember the school years. On the mountain I went to grade 1 and 2 and don't remember anything at all. The other day when I was driving by a field and saw some horses, I remembered grade 6 when I joined a group who were learning about horses. Out of the blue this happened in my head. I could see the classroom that we met in.

I have had amnesia for so many years and no one has even known. I have pretended to be all here and not been. If I can pull off all of what I do and not be all here, I wonder what I would be like if I were really all here. Having amnesia has been a sad thing for me. Not remembering what you've done and even who you are. I get called by a name and I answer. But I do not feel as if the name is really mine. I was known by another name a few years ago and some of my old friends still call me that name. It feels alien to me. I am not her and yet they insist that I am. She played a definite role, got lost inside of the role and maybe that gave her an identity.

I go out there now and do what I know and I do it well. People listen to me and really respect what I have to contribute. When I do this, I feel as if I am someone. But now I feel as if I am in a place between the worlds. That place that I have amnesia or amnesia waking up. Filling in the gaps of my history. I often wonder if there are many people who have blank histories like I do.

The moon will be full again in a week's time. I feel stoned and I don't take anything. I can remember some of the things that happened in the gully. He was a wicked, evil man. He would get turned on to see me in my swim suit. He would take his penis out through his zipper and put it in my mouth. Then he would put it inside of my swim suit. He would rub himself on my clitoris and squirt his semen all over. I felt so dirty and ashamed. He would make me go back to play with the children and he would give me a story to tell them. I've been sitting here holding my hand over my mouth. Holding back the scream. Breathing into myself and not getting lost inside of the pain of the horror. It is like it has just happened to me. I'm spacing off now. This is what I do when I hurt so much. I need to cry. I spent most of my life living like this.

"Why couldn't I have a nice daddy? Why did he have to always do these things to me?"

I'm remembering it and feeling it. I remember. My throat hurts. I want him to go away. Until I disappeared, there was no one left except the part of me who believed that she was only here to be hurt by men.

Today I gave my ex the benefit of the doubt. He never called to say that he was not giving me my maintenance for June so I decided to not jump to conclusions. So I phoned his place and assumed that he had delivered my check to my mailbox and it had gotten stolen. There is this voice inside that says that he did not bring it. But he had said that if he could not he would give me notice and his girlfriend said that he would never stop making the payments, so it must have gotten stolen.

July 16

Where do the days go? So many things have happened to me since I last wrote. I received a letter from my father of origin. I read the letter and then I burned it and the envelope and Flushed them down the toilet. I saw my family Doctor, I was a mess of pain. She suggested that I might like to see someone to talk to. I agreed with her. And so, I will again begin to work on myself. This time I will work on a conscious level around my father. I am choosing to go and work on the relationship that I'd had with him. To remember and embrace the little one and bring her out of the amnesia and back to the now with me.

When I'd read the letter, it triggered some things in me. It was the daddy who used to come to the gravel pit to rescue me and clean up the blood and warm my little body. I would feel so very confused. This same man would take me to the gravel pit and hurt me and then he would go away. Next he would come back and pretend that he'd never been there. He would be so nice to me. When I read this letter that he sent, I again felt the confusion. It did not go with everything that I was remembering. Besides, how could he know what gravel pit to come to, to find me?

Gosh, I just got that. How did he know where to find me? It was night and very dark and late out. I'm waking up in this place right now. He was both of them. And me, I know this. So that must mean that I am both of the *me's* that met both of the *him's*. Only there was just him and just me. I'd become two people to live through this ordeal. One of me got lost from this world because she, I could not compute without short circuiting inside like right now. I am confused and I'm going blank. So this means I need to process and sort this out inside of me.

July 21, 1990

I received some monies from my grandmother. Enough to go out and buy a nice car. I picked it up yesterday. So much to say and I can not sort things this night. Maybe tomorrow I will be able to.

July 22

The weather is very warm and quiet. I feel lazy and sleepy. It is Sunday today. I've been making a list for food to take camping. Some very warm friends of mine are lending me their 22 foot trailer to take up to the lake. We will stay for 6 days, the boys and I. My energy is low. It is the heat and all that I have gone through this past while that is draining me.

Later

I had a really interesting dream the other night. A part of it is I remember my father in it. I said to him that I would make sure that he remembered what he did to me and that he owned it. I was not afraid of him in the dream. I looked in him in his left eye and he backed up because this beam of light zapped him in that eye. It was as if the light was hurting him. He lives in the darkness. When I woke, I was no longer afraid of him. There was much more to this dream, but I can not remember right now.

After the last memory that was released I had to see my family physician. I already told you that, but I did not tell you that I break out in this strange bruise on my stomach. It was the size of a Looney (old fashioned silver dollar) Located between my belly button and my pubic hair.

Maybe because I've been through so much deep integration and pain I'm so blank on many of the memories. It's a good thing I remember the things that I'm doing in the now world. It is as if I don't really have a yesterday, only today and a tomorrow even if tomorrow isn't here yet.

Anna went to the week long summer intensive camp this year. I chose not to attend this time. I don't really know why I decided not to go. Guess I'm not in a place inside of me to go. Yet I find myself thinking of all the great people that I have met the last 2 summers at camp. I sent a copy of the newspaper article with Anna to share with Pandora and Starhawk. I hope she remembered to take it and show it.

July 24, 1990

Time to begin putting down on paper what I have been avoiding. Last Jan. 22, my friend Jerry was here and I was doing her hair for her. I guess a part of her (she is a multiple) decided that I had gotten too close to her. She picked up the scissors that I had used to cut her hair and silently threatened me with them. I acknowledged that she was needing me to not be so close to her. Shortly after this she ended up back in the hospital in the psych. ward. Just prior to valentines day I went up to visit her. At first little Jerry was present because we had a hug. I'd had sent her a wonderful card and it made her begin to cry. Next thing you know, she switches into someone else and says to me that she would get a bigger pair of scissors next time. I backed up and said that I would give her the space that she wanted. She said, "but not too much space".

Since this day I have been very uncomfortable with her. I did do her hair again after she finally was released from the psych. ward. But I made sure that Ron was there so that I was not alone with her. After they got home to their place, she told him that she would probably not see me again and she would find someone new to do her hair. I'm confused about what is happening for me. I'm angry with her for threatening me and I feel as if I am her victim. As if she has some power over me. Like when I was with my ex husband or my father. They would have power over me. One with his physical, sexual, abusive behaviour and the other with his sexual, physical, abusive behaviour.

Again I am frightened for my safety. I know that the reality is that Jerry being someone else would and could hurt me. I'm really pissed off at her, with her. Nice friend eh? Holds up a pair of scissors and waves them around in a threatening way. Not a friend. Friends do not try and hurt each other like that. Maybe I should write her a letter and tell her what a fucking bitch she is. We, I thought had a really deep friendship. All me I suppose. I do not and am not a victim any more and I will not be victim to her. How dare she threaten me. How dare she. I've not had this kind of anger for her before. I have a great deal right now and its for her.

I guess what I have been doing is looking always to her to see where she is at and what is going on for her, trying to figure out what is happening for her and avoiding me. This is what I would always do with the abusive people that I had lived with. Did I trade them for her? When she and I had met we were both in a similar place of fear and childlike place. I grew on past that place and maybe she didn't, I guess it is gone now. But I do not want to forget the anger that I have for her right now. If I do I will be avoiding what I am feeling. I can not be a friend to someone who wishes to harm me. I am angry that I was put in this place of fear. Feeling like her victim has not been a nice feeling. I've even been asking Ron how she is and what she is doing. She always needs to go back to her father. Have I projected a part of me out onto her so that I will never have to go back? Because she always does it.

Another piece of me. So what I need to do is get clear here and not be a victim. Be angry, that is what usually saves me. I need to remove myself from her energy. To say goodbye. She needs to stay in that old place because it is what she likes to do. I need to move on and grow and change. Maybe this is why people like to be with me. I am really angry with her though. I should write and tell her that I felt and feel hurt and angry that she did this to me. Actually I would like to smack her for doing this. It is as if she is her father and herself both. My chest hurts with the pain inside of it. I would like to grab her and shake her and scream at her. This is the first time that I have allowed myself to do this around her. All along

I've projected this power onto her. Well I want my power back that I gave her. (April 6, 2009. I need you to know that this was all in my imagination.)

August 8, 1990

Myself and both of my boys are up at the lake for 5 days. The weather is beautiful and warm. Today I hiked up a nearby hill. It took us (2 of my friends came) 2.5 hours to make the return trip. What to say? I'm at peace right now and feel as if I do not want to work anymore.

When I was talking to one of my friends, I was sharing and remembering being up at the dam. I was held over the edge by both of my ankles and then one was let go of. Only the right ankle was being held onto now. I dropped my doll and she landed against the cement and her head smashed. In my head I could see me going next. The man that was holding onto my ankle was drunk. The grownups were laughing because they thought it was funny. My body went limp. The laughing stopped. It wasn't fun anymore for them. So the man put me back down on the ground. I was not really there any more. An empty body was there. As an adult I wonder how could any person get fun terrifying a small child? I do not understand this.

Today I had a nice day doing the hike and going swimming with my friends. A fire would have been nice tonight. The boys are too busy in their own worlds to think of these things now though. My older son has taken off and forgot that he has my only set of car keys. This makes me feel very uncomfortable. Not having access to a car to get me to where I need to be. This makes me angry that he has done this without thinking.

March 4, 1991 7 months later

Last night I had a dream. This dream was of my father, myself and Donald my brother. I was sitting on the coach with my father on my left side with his arm around me. I was around 12 years of age.

This is the first dream of its kind. I've been doing work on me again, with a psychiatrist. My shoulders are tight, my right hand is numb, my face on the right side is developing tic douloureux again and I want to scream. My neck is tight and it hurts. I need to cry.

My father put his hand inside of my pants and panties. He began to fondle my clitoris. He stuck his finger inside of me. This felt so good. I felt myself getting wet and this excited him. He began to rub his fingers back and forth on the outside of my clitoris. I was feeling so turned on. I just sat there snuggled next to him. We could hear my brother Donald upstairs, he was scrubbing the floor. It felt so neat to have this special attention from my father. As he poked around ever so gently. I did not dare make a sound. I did not want him to stop what he was doing.

All of a sudden he stopped and stood up. He walked over to the stairs and faced my way and began to climb the stairs. I saw that he had an erection and his face looked real mad. He was not looking at me or anyone. He went up the stairs. I felt deserted being left there on the coach with all of these feelings. I began to play with myself. Donald came down the stairs and I quickly pulled up my pants.

We talked about how hard it was to scrub that floor upstairs. The telephone rang and I woke up. All these feelings of being sexually aroused were with me..? I've been feeling somewhat turned on and somewhat angry. Why a dream such as this? What am I to learn??? My body says that it is full of anger. These feelings of pain that I am experiencing. This does not seem real.

I had thoughts of calling Bob or Pharaoh, who a long time ago I did bodywork therapy with. Knowing that on a very close level something incredibly powerful is happening for me. Am I going to integrate my anger for my father?? Is my sexuality connected to what the dream has showed me??

This is what I have to heal? Accept something so repulsive? That I actually liked it when he touched me like that? He didn't always hurt me. I need to see a therapist again. Can this wait until next Wednesday? I do not want to ever get tic douloureux again.

LETTER TO MY FATHER Aug. 16, 1991 (with returned birthday card unopened)

Last fall I wrote you a letter (sent to your condo) explaining the difficult time that I was having. I asked for your support i.e.: financially, you ignored me. I ended up at the welfare office getting a food voucher. My sons do not know this information.

The end of February this year a car smashes into me on the highway. My car is munched in. It's now repaired but it'll take approx. 2 years to repair me. I'm having a bit of an M.S. flare up because of the accident. 100% the other guys fault. I'm on UI disability and managing.

And you send Christmas card and birthday card. What a joke. I don't want your cards.
'Reace

October 14, 1991   7 months later

Today I reread the whole journal. I had been concerned about how it flowed. But it seems to be OK.

Pharaoh popped back into my life. I'm angry with him right now. My world has changed. I'm more open with people now and warmer. Yet with Pharaoh I did not let him know how I felt with what was happening. It was like his agenda was the only one that mattered. This is not true. Mine matters also. I have got some old stuff happening with him.

I went to the Unitarian church on Sunday. I got up and shared during sharing time. What I shared was that it was the first time that I'd been in church since my mother had died in 1985. I was aware of how angry I was with god for taking her from me because I had unresolved business with her. As I did this my whole body trembled. I wanted her to stay alive and tell me why she did those things to me and why she didn't stop him. I wanted her to hold me and love me.

I'm publicly telling people that I am a survivor of satanic ritual abuse. I do not need to hide this. No one can harm me any more. If they tried they would be exposing themselves now. I can't believe I have let happen what happened with Pharaoh. Why did I let him have the power? He even said he didn't like it. I feel as if I've set myself up. Well it is over now because I'm back in my power.

I had a wonderful evening with some people at a friend's stone soup party. People who weren't projecting so strongly on me.

Last week when I did my work with my therapist I did really deep work and now I can't remember what I did. Oh yes I can - It was when my mom died and my dad was back reliving the time his mother died 30 years earlier. He looked at me and said, "Janie, (my mother's name) how could you accuse me of such things on the eve of my mother's death." All I'd said was that I was remembering being sexually abused as a child. After he said this, I said, "Daddy, grandma didn't die, momma died." I had blocked this since mother's death. Many of the cult members attended her service at the church. Some of them approached me and said, I bet you don't remember me. I said. Yes I do and said their name. They were not comfortable. (Interesting that while on this day I could recall all of them by name and then forget completely.)

October 24, 1991

Yesterday was a hard day for me. I saw my therapist first thing in the morning. Up until I saw her, I'd had this pain in my chest that was so strong. It hurt for me to breath. The whole time I was with her I cried. So much pain and so many tears. Halloween is almost here and I remember things that I do not like to remember.

Dark outside, a coffin and someone saying be a good girl and it will be over real soon. I get put in the coffin. I don't like it because there are spiders in it. They close the lid. Everyone is in there dark robes with hoods on them. I feel like I'm watching a movie. I'm outside of myself but yesterday I was inside feeling the pain and the fear. They lower the coffin into the hole in the ground and throw dirt on it. There is a little girl in there you idiots. She is frozen in terror. What the fuck are you doing? What could you jerks possibly get out of such stupidity? Enough of this. You're all retarded. Get out of my way. What planet are you all on anyway? You stupid, ignorant beings. I have only disgust for you all.

Right now I am opening the coffin and helping the little girl out. It is like there is no life inside of her. Now there are tears once more. Tears of sadness and sorrow. That little girl was me. Idiots, your all idiots. No wonder I'm numb today. I was so tired last night. So very tired. My therapist suggested that maybe we weren't in a graveyard because they lock the gates at the graveyards. That maybe we were somewhere else.

This has helped me not be lost in what was happening to me. I'm looking at the surroundings more. But it looks like a graveyard. Maybe I'm not meant to get lost in there again. Feel the pain from this adult place. Integrate the little one into who I am now.

I've spent more time with Pharaoh. I was able to tell him how I had felt. I let him inside of me. I opened up and didn't go away. I was there with him. The first time in my whole life I have let someone inside of me completely. I laughed. I felt wonderful. No masks. Me there. I have many inhibitions to overcome so that I can let go and enjoy. He, Pharaoh makes life so wonderfully light and loving. Even when he is in so much pain himself.

Yesterday, I was sore and bitchy. For awhile I thought I would have to call my therapist and see her again before our next session. But something shifted and I began pulling myself together. Today will be a quiet day for me. It was unfocused anger. It's a good thing that I registered for a anger workshop" for next month. I told my therapist that I feel as if I will spend the rest of my life putting me back together again. She said I probably will.

I have been hoping that I will get a federal appointment for Violence Against Women, but I haven't heard anything yet. I'm still hoping.

The second stage housing program that I developed seems to have ended. Yet I am still facilitating the group meetings for the women. Carrie needed to do a take over and oust me out. Because she had the power as president she could do it. The chance that I took when I turned the power over to her. It was like she became my mother and I got to play out some unfinished business. Carrie was extremely dominating and manipulative. The only way I could survive what she had going on for herself was by removing myself completely. She actually changed the locks on me.

The car accident and my being down physically made it more difficult for me. I couldn't fight. So the concept that I started is still happening with the group that I am facilitating and Carrie had an empty office full of $20,000.00 worth of furnishings and no clients. Crazy. So I learned how to separate myself from my mother's issues that I carried inside of myself, during this whole process. That was worth while. I'm sad that so much was lost though. Someday someone will begin again. It is all documented in my Second Stage Transition Housing document from college. So it will be easier for the next person.

I got to taste rage, thanks to Carrie. Rage is a foul bitter sickening taste. I had never felt safe enough to taste my rage before. So now what do I do. Where does Pharaoh fit in?

October 28, 1991

This afternoon it is snowing outside. It has never snowed this early in the year while I've been alive before. The flakes are beautiful to watch. My mood is weepy this day. So the snow fits.

I want so much to change the horror feelings I get when I'm in a car out in the snow. The blood and the pieces of bodies on the white snow. Whose blood and where did the body pieces come from? Make it different. Go out in the car in the snow and stay present in the now. Easier said than done.

Why am I so emotional? The tears are right here. When Pharaoh was leaving last night, I put my arms around him and hung on. I want so much to be able to believe that someone will be there for me. When I told him that I almost lost it last week and that Halloween was a very bad time for me, he said why didn't you call? Always I have to do things on my own, and to have someone there for me but afraid to have someone there.

My body is reacting to the costumes. Adults in Halloween costumes make my body stiffen up. I remember my mom and dad getting dressed up for a party. They both wore devil outfits. Red tights with tails and red tops and hats with horns. The party when we were up North. Lots of booze and noise. Red blood. An old woman scaring me and me hiding behind my dad. I was so scared. But then I lose the rest of the night. Strange that I never thought to take my life back then. I did try when I was a teen though. My dad stopped me. I never knew why I was crying. I just cried all the time. It drove my mom nuts. My blood down between my legs. It scared me. The little girl that was a part of those violations is very near the surface. I know this because I'm spacey and not all here. I become disoriented and forgetful. There is too much going on inside of me.

My hands have been feeling pins and needles. It started last week after I'd been swimming for awhile. I did 20 lengths and then the needles and pins. An MS symptom. I feel as if I'm going far into unresolved pain and emotions.

Donald called a few days ago. He said that we were different because usually the one that was done to is kicked out of the family alone. We're different because we both left. We both refuse to play a lie. I liked talking to him. He is so grounded in his family life and this gives me an anchor.

So why so much pain around my having Pharaoh for a friend? This I do not understand. I feel confused and unclear inside of me. I need to get my shit together and get focused and well and move back out into the world. Come January /92 I want to be able to head back out there. My direction is unclear right now, but I will again become political or I mean continue to be political. I feel murky. When I see my therapist I will talk about the adults in the costumes and let me feel what my body remembers.

I never told you who Pharaoh is. 8 years ago when I'd first left my abusive marriage, I began doing my own personal therapy. The first year I worked with Bob, well part of the first year. In the spring of 1984, I went to a holistic workshop and Pharaoh was one of the facilitators. A month later I started working with him and still with Bob. At one workshop I told Pharaoh he was the first man that I'd ever trusted. There was lots of love and lots of transference. Yet a friendship was kindled. Always there was something in the connection for me with him and I now see for him with me. He felt close enough to reach out to me almost 5 years later. Before I was emotionally young and now the years have aged me. Lots of growth and changes for me. I will eventually get clear in this place. The young part of me comes here with Pharaoh. She stays in the shadows but she is here.

Oct. 30

When my brother called, he was an anchor for me into my now life. Today I worked with my therapist and explored my feelings around Pharaoh. It seems that I, me, my body does trust him. I find this curious. This is short circuiting me, my willingness to let someone inside of me so deeply. A new level for me.

Dec. 9, 1991

Hi, it's me. This is weird, I sit here and begin to do this and the tears come to my eyes and I feel choked up. Too much has happened. This is not going to be easy. Taking a deep breath right now. My chest is hurting.

I went to the anger workshop a few weeks ago. At this workshop I allowed the little one inside of me to bring her anger forth around the satanic ritual abuse. Seems I'm holding on right now. How to tell you some of the things that I personally experienced without me coming unglued.

My therapist prescribed some medication for me to help slow things down a bit. Now I'm hot. I go blank and have a stunned feeling. Like right now and I haven't taken anything. I don't know how to tell you or help you understand or feel some of what I had to see and do. My adult life is making more sense now. All of the strange notions that I get. Now I find me looking out the window at the clouds. Always trying to distract or to run away.

When I was 27 they took my uterus out. I'd been bleeding so heavy that I would faint from the loss of blood. They found my womb full of scar tissue. When I was a little girl the grown ups would make me lick a woman between her legs when she was bleeding. The smell was awful. I wanted them to take my uterus out, I hated it. I hated it when I bled between my legs. My head hurts right now. There was a full moon service and it was very important. I was the star of the ritual. Satan's daughter in the circle. I have a friend and she is a lesbian. She doesn't know that I'm afraid of her. She is a nice woman and I respect her work. She is a counsellor with similar philosophy to mine. Maybe I can make it different by telling her. Now I start to cough. Goddess how my body reacts to everything.

One of the dances that we did at the anger workshop was the dark side. We were to be hunting for the little children and I said that when I was little these things really did happen. I began to lose it.

I felt like a trapped animal and ran to another room and paced back and forth because there was no where to go. I was trapped. What I would have done then was switch to someone else but one of the women from the group followed me and put her arms around me and held me. One of the leaders came in and saw that I was in trouble. She asked me if I could put my arms around the woman that was holding me and I did. She then talked me into breathing. I didn't go away. I stayed here. Part of me went back there but not all of me.

Since this workshop I can look at new baby girls and not be afraid of them. I can see them. I never was able to attend anything special that adults put on for baby girls. Birthday parties, things like that. Not until they were older could I touch them.

The cult would sacrifice infant girls to Satan. Everyone would drink their blood. Everyone. They said I was his daughter and that I was very important. I was his special girl. And one day I would grow up and become married to him.

When my mother died I went into her bedroom and took her ring and put it on my wedding finger. I looked down at what I'd done and took it off. When my mother died my father put his mouth on mine and I ran from the room. I did not want what was supposed to be.

I never see my father of origin any more. I'm not afraid of him either. I don't want him in my life. He is a horrible person.

When little babies disappear around Halloween and Thanksgiving or Christmas, my insides tell me that they came and got them. They are gone now. Poor little babies. I have lots of dolls from when I was a little girl and I remember being a good mom and looking after them because I wasn't like those grownups.

Sometimes I feel a little insane. I've let an hour go by and come back. Last Friday when I was going into the city with a friend I just began to blurt out things around what I've been remembering lately.

I talked about some services where little children were eaten. I got lost for a bit. I asked him to talk and it helped me get back here in this world. After that I had a very nice evening. About babies being born right there and then killed. It didn't matter because nobody knew that they were even here anyway. I remember hearing this being said. No wonder I went numb. How could anyone stay here on a conscious level and be a part of these things?

One day I will come out of shock and out of numbness and feel alive completely. I'm just beginning to realize how much more of me is still in amnesia. When I saw my therapist two weeks ago, I was having a flood of hallucinations and visions that were making me crazy. This is when she suggested that I have some help. Just slow things down and have them come at a pace I can not lose my mind with.

Dec. 27, 1991

I'm over on the island right now. I got here at 11:30 am this morning. Went for a walk to the beach after I unpacked. I told people that I didn't know if I would come back on Mon., Tue.., or Wed.. I'll see how it goes for me. I'm already feeling the quiet of the Island. Deep breathing and sighing. Letting go of the stress of the mainland. I brought the dog with me.

I like spending time alone with me. I hope I get a call and an interview for this job that I applied for. I want this position.

The session after I wrote the last entry, I took what I'd wrote and shared it with my therapist, I was halfway down the first page and the emotion became so strong. I stayed here and read the whole thing. (Did not switch to another personality) It was like my sharing it made it real. I told someone and she listened.

A day or so after I'd read my last entry to my therapist, I had this dream. The dream was of this person and I going out and cutting people and drinking their blood. In the dream this person who became a man wanted to slit this guys throat. This guy was in a comatose state like he was drugged. I stopped him from doing this and showed him another way to get a lot of blood without killing the guy. I was very clear in the dream and I was drinking and sampling the different bloods. I would take a razor sharp, I just had a break through, the instrument that we would use to cut the people was a medical one. One of those things they use in surgery. I can see it as clear as day right now. I became very skilled at cutting the people for their blood. We actually developed a taste for the blood. I feel spaced out right now, like I'm not me or me who I was the other day.

It's dark outside now. I can hear the waves below. I'd decided that I wanted to begin closing this journal while I was on the Island. There is enough information for the medical population to learn some things in what I've already written. I know that my journey is a long way from completion. As my life is a long way from being over. I keep going blank and maybe I'll keep going blank for the rest of my life. Sometimes I wonder if I'll ever retrieve completely, my memories of my youth.

It is wonderful that I created alternates. My friend Pharaoh has me confused. He would say, what's confusing and be precise in what he was meaning. So I guess it is me who is confusing me. I don't like his switching. He can get mean. I don't like his switching. I feel like he has this concept of who I am and it is not me. I get really confused when I think of him when I'm in this place that I'm in right now. I'm not clear and to relate with him I need to be clear so I don't take on his projections. Why do I only experience this with him? I don't feel grounded in the solid material world when I'm with him. I don't feel I'm in my power, that I'm anchored inside of me when I'm with him. I just got that.

Dec. 28, 1991

My dreams are my unconscious opening up to me, my past. I went hiking for awhile this day. It is so beautiful out. The magic is strong and I feel tranced.

I was thinking about how I ran and hid inside of the church to get away from my abusive husband. And now I avoid it like it were the plague. I do not feel free inside of the church. I feel as if I were a trapped animal. I've run away from god. Like the dream I had years ago. Me being prepared to meet my mate and as I was being taken to him, I ran. I ran out into the world full of people to get lost. Yet an old woman saw me and stood still with her walking stick and said to me, child, you can not run away from your destiny. I've been running ever since. Yet the life I've lived is catching up to me. On one hand I run and on the other, I work hard to find my life. Always being torn in two. People confuse me. All of the energy out in the world makes me dizzy. The old woman also said, you can not hide.

I like being on the Island. It is so peaceful here. Yet I am different now. I've come to this Island for years and just now I allow people into my space. But I'm feeling crowded again. So many people and not enough space for me. So much energy inside of me. So many thoughts are swarming inside of me, so many memories being released. That's why I feel dizzy. It takes me awhile but I eventually, well almost find out what is happening inside of me. I've slept a lot last night and today. I got up at 8:30 and went back to bed twice after that.

When we left the city when I was 5 years old there was an urgency in my parents and there were others that left when we did. Did they come close to getting found out? Who did they kill? Why did we leave everything behind and run and hide on the mountain? Do I want to really remember? Is it going to be any more difficult to integrate than what I've already seen in my mind's eye? There is this scream inside of me, like I want to tear my body apart and fling the pieces everywhere and just scream and cry. Will I get clear?

The men in my life say they see a shield around me. I can't let go. I won't give me away. I'll share me but not give me away.

The waves sound beautiful right now. A big boat just went by and made them. Maybe I need to let myself go through the fear of being locked inside of a church or contained against my will by another human to get past this claustrophobic feeling that I always get.

Dec. 30, 1991

A correction. A man in my life says he sees a shield. Maybe it's because I don't feel safe yet.

Yesterday was a difficult day for me. So much happening inside of me. Today I feel frustration. I'm having difficulty remembering what I did before today. I'm trying to make Pharaoh go away inside of me... He said that I have to let him go. That he is unhealthy for me. He's got that right. I find him abrasive, abusive, controlling, confusing, bossy, and I think he is mirroring all of the qualities that are in me. I really don't think that I'm as extreme as he is. So maybe I need to polish myself. So this is how I make people who are mean to me go away. I see what is bothering me in them and then I take it inside of me and own it. I was totally off center yesterday when Pharaoh called. He is not a supportive person in my world. He connected with me only because he needed support. What a sucker I am. I should have charged him for the connection. Like he did to me years ago when I called him for support and he charged me $50.00 for the hour on the telephone. This I've never done to anyone of my friends. Maybe he should be reported for his unethical manners.

I'm learning how not to be by my experiences of other so called professionals. Yesterday I was in a victim place. I'm so glad that my real friend Ronny called after Pharaoh did. Ron listened to my tears and did not take on my stuff or mix his with mine. This is what a supportive friendship is. Pharaoh was quick to project everything onto me. Why not, if I was willing to take it. He also said that he didn't find me very open to him, I was desperately trying to protect myself. At one point I felt like hanging up the phone. I wish that I had done this.

Pharoah was just as supportive as he was when I had my car accident. How can he be here for me when he can't be here for himself? It takes me awhile but I finally get it. He says he doesn't want my negative energy. This is what he has invited.

I'm feeling crushed. Like I've lost my power and have become a person who is groveling to get inside. How did I get outside of life. It's like people have taken something from me and I want it back. I'm mentally clawing people's eyes out to try and get back what they took away from me. I need to rise above this. If it's so important for them to take something of mine then I should let go because they think that they obviously need it. They still don't have me. I can't let them know that I've been crushed. I need to find my power so that I can return to the outside world and not get eaten alive.

Women are just as abusive as men are. Some women that I know who work in transition houses and think that they're doing good for other women are they themselves abusive. I feel used and abused by Pharoah. So am I going to be a victim again? I'm afraid of him. When I feel like a victim I'm on the outside of my life. I leave my body and run away. This is not safe.

So much of my old world has come into my new world and I'm finding it hard to hang onto me in the new. Is the medication that my therapist prescribed to me, helping? Why am I fighting so hard? Why do I find it so difficult to believe that Pharoah could actually be an abusive man. He confuses me the way my father confused me. He's more than one person. And I continually give him power and appreciation for giving me opportunities for advancement. What a hoot.. Always I look for the good in human beings. I turn the ugly into something positive for me. I really am crazy.

I don't get to see my therapist until next week. How sane will I be by then?

The ego is powerful. Who really is to say which world we live in is the world of advancement? They all have opportunity for advances. Show us the way?? The Way. Whose Way?? Everyone is looking for a way. Always outside of the self. It's hilarious. I'm really inside of me now eh?

December 31, 1991

I need you to know, when Pharaoh charged me the $50.00 for the phone call, he was my therapist. Maybe this is why they say that when you've done therapy with someone you can never have a personal relationship with that someone. I've obviously done a transference with him. And, he with me. It takes adults to move beyond this. I read back a ways and discovered that at the beginning of the year I'd said that I'd needed to see Pharaoh or Bob. All around sexuality. My feeling in that place a long time ago with my father of origin. Interesting that Pharaoh arrived in my life so that I could bring back to life that part of me I'd rejected so long ago. Pharaoh said that everything changed after that night we made love and that he never wanted it to happen again. For me it was the most wonderful night of my life. I was brought back to life in a very vulnerable place. Maybe now I'm just taking too much of his stuff on. I'll respect what he has said to me. Not to call him again until I'm clear. He never wants to have sex with me again. That we made a mistake by changing our relationship to include sex. I finished by asking that he return my things before he moves.

Late yesterday afternoon I went for physio on the island. I met the most marvellous woman. She does hands on. I experienced her as working with energy in my body, some energy balancing and working with the bones. Afterwards I felt so relaxed and present in the now. Clear and strong within myself. I'm seeing her again this Thursday. Rolfing, that's what it was.

January 1, 1992

When I was coming from the mountain, my parents decided to play straight. We all were placed inside of a church and told to join everything that we were eligible for. When I was inside the church my father would be that wonderful father. I used to play make believe, so much that I was very connected to the pretend world. It became the only world that I lived in and now I feel locked up in the world of the church. I need to go through these things so that I can find out what it is that terrifies me so. Then the torture will come to an end.

I know that the dream that I'd had about learning how to cut people and get their blood, was my subconscious releasing a memory. I did drink the blood of humans. My dreams are all from my subconscious and when I'm strong enough to bring them into reality... This is when I remember in today.

March 26, 1992

I'm closing this section of my journal now. Pharaoh and I were able to clear with each other. We were lovers again and it was beautiful. I've found my power in our relationship. I'm separate from him now. Thank you Pharaoh for your love and tenderness.

A new door has opened for me. The door into my teenage self. I relived my father of origin anal raping me when I was 14 years old. "Must not get her pregnant again". Seems things did not stop at that time for me. Yet I left amnesia for a part of my life in my teen years. I actually have memories of a life outside of my family home. (I have few memories from inside the home) I had friends. They were mostly from the same world that I lived in at home. The girls were all abused by their dads. But back then, I wasn't. They sensed something in me and were (the girls) protective towards me.

I ran from myself and into trouble.

9 months later

I reread my journal in preparation for, in hopes of, publishing. I am sitting back on the island in front of the fire. I am proud of myself for surviving, for getting past surviving. I know that I am going to be a part of opening the door of reality to Satanic Ritual Abuse on this planet in my first hand knowledge, I know I am a valuable asset. But mostly the healing world as I've recovered from having had Multiple Sclerosis.

My nightmares are strong again. My subconscious releases my memories of my past this way. I'm remembering little children being murdered and eaten. I am forced to watch and participate in the murder. My friend was brown skinned and retarded. I didn't want him to die. I loved my friend.

In the night I wake feeling little and very young and go to another room and curl up in a little ball praying that the next murder won't be mine. Will I ever be able to live in peace?

My father is dying and my rightful place would be to become high priestess. I choose to take this power and knowledge and come out into the world and not get lost in the cult. It is my sincere hope that in sharing my story others will see that it is possible to find their way out from the darkness into the light.

I feel ripped off. Ripped off of a life, the life of the little girl who was not allowed to be. Why? Why wouldn't they let her be? I feel as if I didn't get to experience being alive. I wasn't there, not me anyway. I want her to be! My kids got a raw deal also. I was so out of it when they were little. Having multiple sclerosis and taking drugs (drug store and street) I missed so much. Yes, I feel ripped off of life. And all because I had to turn off the lights just so I could survive. Some people are weird!! There are lots of sickos out there.

Namaste'
'Reace

A HEALING JOURNEY

'Reace entered psychotherapy in 1983. Her marriage had recently disintegrated and she was left to care for her two young children on her own.

She had lost her direction and purpose in life and appeared dissociated, disconnected, distressed, scared and guarded. She also exhibited physical symptoms of multiple sclerosis, such as numbness in her legs and blurred or double vision. She walked with a cane at times and wore a patch over one eye on occasion.

During the first year of therapy, 'Reace remained aloof and wouldn't let me get close to her. She was terrified of men as a result of having been abused, most recently by her husband and before that, by her father.

During the second year of therapy, 'Reace began to trust, open her heart, and share her deeper feelings and experiences with me. She allowed me to hold her while she cried and released the stress in her body.

As time passed, 'Reace began to connect with the painful feelings associated with the thoughts and images emanating from her psyche. She got in touch with traumatic events from her childhood, and in working through her trauma, 'Reace encountered the ghosts of her past who tormented her. Together, we confronted them through open dialogue, exploration of her personal mythology (that is the stories she told herself about her childhood experiences), family patterns, and patterns in relationship. We also processed through gestalt therapy, hypnosis, dream work, music and breath work, and body work.

The body work, which consisted of deep tissue massage and bio-energetics, was an indispensable part of this process. As 'Reace released the feelings which were trapped in contracted muscles by yelling, screaming, kicking and crying; and confronted the images and associations which were connected with these feelings, her healing progressed further. Blood flow reached areas previously blocked by contractions and she was able to breathe more openly.

Her multiple sclerosis symptoms disappeared within the first three years of therapy, and only reappeared briefly twelve years later during a time of intense stress. She felt more whole and less dissociated and disjointed.

Music and breath work also contributed to 'Reace's healing by creating an altered state in which the unconscious become conscious and was then processed therapeutically in session. Further healing occurred when 'Reace began to pursue the practice of yoga, which contributed to her sense of physical and emotional well being and stability. The stretching and opening of muscles, along with the deep breathing which she engaged in while practicing yoga, induce a calming effect, which grounded her, as did the self acceptance that was engendered and supported in psychotherapy.

The one eye integration work with Dr. Bradshaw has been another important aspect of 'Reace's healing; in that it too led to her feeling less dissociated, and more connected to her feelings and thoughts.

In summary, I believe that 'Reace's psychological and physical symptoms were, in large part, caused by psychologically and /or physically traumatic events. In other words, whatever the congenital pre disposition that existed within 'Reace, there appears to have been a very definite psychosomatic component to her "dis-ease".

Furthermore, 'Reace's psychological and physical healing consisted both physical and psychological components or approaches. This can be clearly seen in the use of body work, yoga, breath and music work and one eye integration work.

Physically, multiple sclerosis is defined by the presence of multiple lesions caused by plaque which impairs normal neural activity, sight and movement. Similarly the multiple wounds cause by psychological events caused 'Reace to experience great emotional distress. When this emotional distress threatened to overwhelm her she dissociated and disconnected from it and the triggering events, in order to survive. You might say that this caused a lesion which, while self inflicted, caused her to disconnect from her conscious awareness of the triggering traumatic events and their accompanying emotions. This, in turn, I believe, contributed to the onset of the multiple sclerosis symptoms, since the traumatic emotions' and accompanying images, remained trapped in chronically contracted muscles and tissues and compressed joints, causing undue stress to her physical system.

I believe that the combined effect of psychological and physical stress on symptom formation manifested itself when 'Reace experienced a brief recurrence of double vision twelve years into her healing journey. A month before the outbreak of this symptom, 'Reace experienced both physical and psychological stress. She had entered into a very emotionally stressful intimate relationship and she also was involved in a motor vehicle accident which resulted in her experiencing soft tissue damage. 'Reace believes that the motor vehicle accident triggered the release of subliminal trauma which later manifested in her M. S. symptoms. I believe, along with her, that her new and stressful intimate relationship was also a contributing factor.

At the time of this writing, 'Reace's healing journey has been a long and very successful one. While her struggles in life continue, as it does for all of us, she had been free from the gross symptoms of multiple sclerosis such as numbness and blurred or double vision for the past 20 years, with the exception of the one month interval mentioned in the last paragraph.

She faces her challenges with more energy, openness, honesty and hope. She seems more self accepting, grounded and adjusted. The number of therapy sessions with 'Reace has decreased over the years from once or twice a week to once every three or four weeks. We are like old friends who have taken a journey in healing together. I feel privileged to have known 'Reace and to have been a part of her healing journey. I am happy for 'Reace and wish her well.

Sincerely,
Bob Berger, M.S.W. , R.S.W., B.C.A.S.W.